THE SOUVENIR GUIDE TO THE BURRELL COLLECTION

by

Richard Marks
Keeper of the Burrell Collection

RICHARD DREW PUBLISHING GLASGOW

First published 1985
Reprinted November 1985, June 1987 and September 1988 by
RICHARD DREW PUBLISHING LIMITED
6 CLAIRMONT GARDENS
GLASGOW G3 7LW
SCOTLAND

British Library Cataloguing in Publication Data
Marks, Richard
   The souvenir guide to the Burrell Collection
   1. Burrell Collection — Guide-books
   I. Title
   708.2'91443   N1315

   ISBN 0-86267-096-9

Printed in Great Britain by
The Eagle Press plc
Blantyre, Scotland

CONTENTS

*Cover illustration: The north side of the Burrell Collection gallery at night.
Photograph by Alastair Hunter.*

1 Sir William Burrell (1861-1958)   *This photograph was taken by the well-known Glasgow firm of photographers, T & R Annan, when Burrell was aged about sixty. It is one of the few photographs of Sir William Burrell, an intensely private man, who resolutely refused to sit for a portrait to be placed in the gallery. He used to say:*
    'The collection, not the collector, is the important thing.'

FOREWORD

The astounding success of the Burrell Collection has been particularly gratifying to Glasgow District Council, the Burrell Trustees and members of staff.

The need for an economically priced guide leading the many visitors from gallery to gallery is overwhelming to complement the present excellent publication which describes the Collection by subject.

The intention of this Souvenir Guide is to take visitors round the galleries in a helpful and constructive way so that their time is not wasted and the experience of seeing a great Collection is a pleasurable one.

I hope that this short Guide, so ably written by Dr Richard Marks, Keeper of the Burrell Collection, will whet visitors' appetites to return many times to the gallery and to study these unique items in an atmosphere of comfort and friendliness.

Art Gallery & Museum,   Alasdair A. Auld
Kelvingrove   DIRECTOR
GLASGOW G3 8AG   *June 1985*

INTRODUCTION

This book acts as a descriptive guide through the Burrell Collection gallery and thus complements the larger publication, *The Burrell Collection*, which gives the artistic and historical context to the various sections of the Collection. The Guide contains many views of the gallery and colour illustrations of the objects in the Collection which are published for the first time.

Because of the gallery's imaginative layout, a tour cannot be straightforward, and inevitably there will be a considerable amount of darting hither and thither. It is not possible, for example, to describe a route in which all the stained glass can be seen in sequence. But the itinerary laid out here is only a suggestion and does not have to be followed; by use of the plans and of the index at the end of the book, one can easily locate rooms of particular interest and find one's way to them.

Two points should be borne in mind when using this Guide. Firstly, not all the items described in the book will be on display all the time. There are more than 8 000 items in the Collection and at any given moment between a quarter and a third of them are on view. This is a high proportion for any museum to show of its total holdings; nevertheless the intention is to change the displays from time to time. A number of the objects are, however, of such importance or interest that it is unlikely that they will be withdrawn from the galleries, other than for conservation purposes or loan to temporary exhibitions elsewhere. The textiles, however, are likely to be changed at regular intervals, if only for conservation reasons (they suffer damage if hung and exposed to light for too long). As it can take up to two years to prepare a single carpet or tapestry for display it is a matter of taking one down and substituting another rather than making wholesale changes in these galleries. Moreover in the Temporary Exhibition area displays, often arranged on a thematic basis or concentrating on specific sections of the Collection, can frequently be seen; this avoids too much disruption to the main galleries.

Secondly the Burrell Collection gallery is fully air-conditioned to allow the temperature and humidity control essential for the preservation of the objects. For the same reason the lighting in the rooms where textiles and prints and drawings are exhibited has to be kept at a low level. This unavoidably reduces visibility, and visitors should allow time for their eyes to adjust to the levels of lighting in these spaces. Again for conservation reasons visitors are earnestly requested not to touch any of the exhibits, even those which seem the most durable.

That the Collection was formed by one individual was very much taken into account when planning the layout. For this reason there is a uniformity of display throughout the various sections and spaces: the walls are painted grey, except in the Hutton Castle and Period Rooms, one neutral colour of fabric is used for mounting and the labels all conform to the same design and typeface.

The most gratifying task for any author in writing an Introduction should be the acknowledgements. My colleagues Jimmy Thomson, Shelagh McPherson and Philip Vainker contributed the individual captions to the objects illustrated from the Ancient Civilizations, Oriental Art and the Pictures respectively; they also suggested valuable amendments and improvements to the text, as did Winnie Tyrrell. I am deeply grateful to the Burrell conservators, Janet Notman, Bill McHugh, Valerie Blyth, Graeme Cannon, Linda Fraser and Sheila Phipps; without their continuous care and attention there would be no Collection to show. Also to Frank Layden and Murdo MacDonald for their work, not least in the moving of the Collection into the present building from its former location. As for the labours involved in typing this manuscript only Louise Devlin, Winnie Tyrrell and Linda Simi can speak: I can only admire their tact, forebearance and transcription skills.

Except for those individually acknowledged, all the photographs used in this book were taken by the photographic section of Glasgow Museums and Art Galleries: Jim Stewart, Ellen Howden, Ina Graham, Maureen Kinnear and Rowan Main; the quality of their work is self-evident. So too is that of Sandy Hamilton, the designer of the book, who has also contributed much to the appearance of the displays and publications of the Burrell Collection. Finally I cannot close without taking the opportunity to thank all the staff, the curators and conservators, the education, security, cleaning, catering and services personnel and everyone else who has worked so hard to make the Collection a success. Particular mention also must be made of certain former members of the Burrell staff: my predecessor Bill Wells, Deborah Carthy, Tony Fitzclarence, Flora Ritchie and Romie Scott.

Richard Marks

THE BURRELL COLLECTION TABLE OF CHIEF EVENTS

1 1861   9 July: William Burrell born in Glasgow

1875   William Burrell joins the family shipping firm of Burrell & Son

1885   On death of their father he and his brother George take over management of Burrell & Son

1899   William Burrell elected to the Council of Glasgow Corporation and becomes convenor of a sub-committee on health

1901   Glasgow International Exhibition: William Burrell the largest single lender. He marries Constance Mitchell

1902   The Burrells move into 8 Great Western Terrace, Glasgow, which had been re-modelled for them by their close friend Robert Lorimer. Birth of their daughter Marion

1911   William Burrell starts recording his acquisitions in Purchase Books

1913-16   Sale of almost all of the Burrell & Son fleet

1916   Burrell buys Hutton Castle. Work commences on alterations under the direction of Robert Lorimer

1923   Burrell appointed Trustee of the National Galleries of Scotland

1927   Burrell moves into Hutton Castle. Knighted for his services to art in Scotland and public works. Appointed a Trustee of the National Gallery of British Art (now the Tate Gallery)

1944   Sir William and Lady Burrell donate the Collection to the City of Glasgow. He continues acquiring works of art

1946   Sir William Burrell gives Glasgow £450,000 to meet the costs of the gallery to house the Collection.

1948   Search for a suitable site in progress

1957   22 June: last entries in the Purchase Books

1958   29 March: death of Sir William Burrell

1961   15 August: death of Lady Burrell

1967   Pollok House and Estate presented to Glasgow by Mrs Maxwell Macdonald and the Trustees of the Burrell Collection agree to housing it in Pollok Park

1972	The architectural competition for the design of the gallery won by Barry Gasson, John Meunier and Brit Andreson
1975	*Treasures from the Burrell Collection* exhibition at the Hayward Gallery, London
1976	The Secretary of State for Scotland announces a substantial grant towards the cost of the gallery
1978	4 May: Miss Burrell inaugurates work on the site
1983	21 October: The Burrell Collection gallery declared open by Her Majesty the Queen
	Barry Gasson awarded the Gold Medal for Architecture by the Royal Scottish Academy
1984	28 April: 500,000th visitor to the Collection
1984	12 September: 1,000,000th visitor to the Collection

The Burrell Collection wins the following awards:

(1) British Tourist Authority *Come to Britain* trophy for 1983

(2) Stone Federation Award for Natural Stone 1983

(3) Award for efficient use of energy from the Chartered Institution of Building Services

Barry Gasson awarded the OBE

The leading tourist attraction in Scotland

1985 Further awards won

(1) 1985 Museum of the Year Award

(2) Scottish Museum of the Year Award

(3) Sotheby's Award for the best Fine Art Museum

(4) Scottish Museum of the Year Award for the best museum publication

USEFUL INFORMATION

Admission

Admission is free and the Burrell Collection is open throughout the year except Christmas Day and New Year's Day.

Opening Times: Monday to Saturday   10am-5pm
                      Sunday   2pm-5pm

How to Get There

The Burrell Collection gallery is set in the delightful surroundings of Pollok Park, about 10 minutes walk from Pollok House.

There is ample car parking space and there are buses from the city centre to the Pollokshaws Road entrance of the park about 20 minutes walk from the gallery. In addition Central Scottish Services run a bus service (no. 908) direct to the Burrell Collection from Anderston Bus Station in Glasgow on Wednesdays and Sundays.

By Bus:

From the city centre - 45, 48A and 57

Across south of city - 34, 89 and 90

From Anderston Bus Station – 908 (for further information telephone 041-248 7432).

By Rail:

Travel from Glasgow Central to Pollokshaws West station or Shawlands station.

Education Services

The Museum Education Service is administered by the Local Education Authority and offers the following:

Teaching service for schools

In service/in-training courses for teachers

Further Education programmes

For information contact:

The Museum Education Officer: Tel: 041-334 1131
                                              041-649 9929

Guided Tours

There are daily conducted tours of the Collection. The times of the tours are announced on the Notice Board in the Courtyard. The service is organized by Glasgow Art Gallery and Museums Association; it is free and no advance booking is necessary.

Facilities for the Handicapped

There are two reserved parking spaces close to the entrance and wheelchairs are available on request for use in the gallery. All areas of the gallery open to the public can be reached by lift and the lavatories are equipped for the disabled.

Cassette audio-guides for the visually handicapped are available from the Enquiry Desk.

Catering

The gallery has a self-service restaurant and a licensed bar.

Study Facilities

Items not on display and the records of the Collection are normally accessible to advanced students and specialists. Advance notice must be given.

Overnight accommodation is available for visiting scholars; preference will be given to those coming from overseas. This must be booked well in advance.

Photographic Services

In addition to the postcards, reproductions and slides on sale in the Shop, photographs and slides of items in the Collection can be ordered. Price lists and order forms are available.

Reminders

1. NO SMOKING IS PERMITTED
2. DO NOT TOUCH THE EXHIBITS

Details and further information from:
The Burrell Collection, Pollok Country Park, 2060 Pollokshaws Road, Glasgow G43 1AT. Tel: 041-649 7151

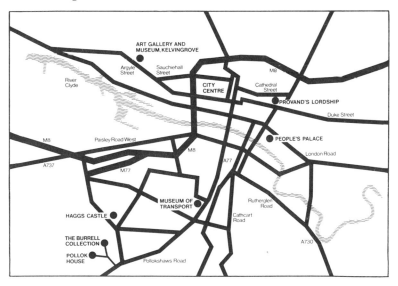

THE SOUVENIR GUIDE

Although this guide is primarily concerned with the Collection proper rather than with its architectural setting, the latter is worthy of study in its own right. It is a modern design, but one which neither detracts from its position in the landscape nor overwhelms the objects displayed within. Indeed its position in the corner of the field and against woodland enables it to make full use of the natural possibilities presented by the site. From the west, the gallery gradually unfolds against the line of trees. The glass walls on the north and south sides reflect the surroundings and permit a continuous interplay between art and nature. The entrance arm and the east wall, with their cladding of red sandstone from Locharbriggs in Dumfries-shire, harmonize well with the exteriors of so many of the handsome Victorian and Edwardian tenement houses in Glasgow. The only item from the Collection displayed outside the building is the 17th-century sundial from Meggatland House in Midlothian.

The gallery is entered through the great oak double doors and sandstone arch in the façade. The arch comes from Hornby Castle in Yorkshire and dates from the 14th century. The creatures carved on the stonework belong to a long tradition of animal carving in Yorkshire sculpture. Only the carved stones are original; the remainder are from Cat's Castle Quarry in Gloucestershire and were cut when the arch was built into the gallery.

2 *The entrance arm and south side in winter.*

3 *The glazed north wall in autumn.   Photograph by Alastair Hunter*

4 Model of the SS Strathclyde   *One of the first vessels ordered by Burrell and Son when the firm was under the management of William Burrell and his brother George. The ship was built in 1889 by Alexander Stephen and Sons of Linthouse. Made of steel, she was powered by triple expansion engines and had a gross tonnage of 3265.*

Inside, the long and narrow Entrance Arm extends from the Lavatories and Cloakrooms to the Enquiry Desk and Shop. On the wall near the Shop is the plaque commemorating the opening of the gallery by Her Majesty the Queen on 21 October 1983 and nearby are several awards made to the Burrell Collection. On the opposite side is a Pay-phone and Letterbox, and adjacent to the Enquiry Desk is a wall-panel giving a brief account of Sir William Burrell and the Collection. A model of one of his ships, the *SS Strathclyde*, is a reminder of the source of the wealth which enabled Burrell to form such a large and comprehensive collection.

5 *The Hutton Castle Dining Room looking east.*

Just beyond the Shop, under the stairs, is the first doorway into the HUTTON CASTLE DINING ROOM. This room, along with the Drawing Room and Hall (see pp.23-26, 82-84), comes from Hutton Castle, Sir William and Lady Burrell's home near Berwick-on-Tweed. They were the most important rooms in the Castle and give a vivid impression of the Burrells' lifestyle. One of Burrell's conditions to the donation of his collection to the City of Glasgow in 1944 was that they should all be reproduced in the new gallery. The rooms are arranged as they were furnished by him in the 1920s and early 1930s with antique furniture, all of it purchased by Burrell from various sources. The rooms also contain the modern furnishings which were specially designed or chosen as a suitable setting for the ancient furniture – velvet curtains, window seats and lampshades, chandeliers and candelabra, as well as wooden pelmets and radiator fronts appropriately carved in an early 16th-century style. There are details of Hutton Castle on the information board on the north (Courtyard side) wall of the Dining Room.

5   The DINING ROOM walls are covered by a series of elaborately-carved *oak panels* dating from *c.*1500. The shield of arms over the contemporary stone fireplace is that of the Copledyke family of Harrington Hall in Lincolnshire, from where the panelling originally came. Displayed on the panelling are 15th-century **tapestry altar frontals**. That on the Courtyard side depicting St Gotthard, Bishop of Hildesheim, and St Pancras bears the arms of the Nuremberg patrician Martin Haller (d.1468) and his wife, Barbara Prunsterin. The largest represents the Coronation of the

Virgin accompanied by five saints, three of whom (Erbanus, Adelarius and Bonifacius) were venerated at Erfurt in Germany, where the tapestry was probably woven. In the heads of the windows are fourteen English shields of arms. The pair in the first window on the left facing into the Courtyard are very early examples of **English heraldic glass**. They depict the royal arms and the arms of the Clare family and date from the late 13th or early 14th century.

In the centre of the room is a large Elizabethan *oak refectory table* with a parquetry top and carved bulbous legs, and a series of *oak armchairs* of the late 16th and early 17th centuries are arranged around it. More oak chairs, including a Scottish piece dated 1689, and several **oak buffet cupboards** and other 16th-century furniture are set against the panelling. Placed on this furniture are a number of *objets d'art*, including **Late Gothic sculptures and candlesticks**. The furnishings of the room are completed by a few items of

6 The Warwick Vase   *Roman, with 18th-century reconstruction work on 2nd-century* A.D. *original   Marble, height 2·94m (9ft 8in)   Reg. no. 42/20   Photograph by Keith Gibson*

Oriental and Near Eastern art, the largest being the 19th-century *Persian flower-pattern carpet*, upon which the large table stands.

The Hutton Dining Room is on the south side of the COURTYARD. The walls of this large space are clad in Locharbriggs stone and the pine roof beams and Portland limestone floor slabs and plinths are typical of the high-quality natural materials used in the construction of the gallery. Distributed around the Courtyard and drawn from a wide range of cultures are a few objects which serve as a suitable introduction to the

6 Collection. The centre is occupied by the majestic *Warwick Vase*, which was discovered in fragments at Tivoli near Rome in 1771. It was presented by Sir William Hamilton, the British Envoy to the Court of Naples, to his nephew George, the second Earl of Warwick.

The Vase represents the Ancient World of Greece and Rome; a flavour of the riches of the Oriental art in the Collection (see pp.26-33, 84-86, 91) is provided by the three Chinese porcelain fish-bowls dating from the late 16th and early 17th centuries A.D., on the north side of the Courtyard. On the east side, beyond the Warwick Vase, are four 12th-century Romanesque capitals set on modern limestone columns and bases. Two of them are probably southern French; the third is from the south of England and is similar to a fine series of capitals from Hyde Abbey, Winchester. The last capital is either French or Italian.

A more dramatic representative of Burrell's medieval interests is

7 the *Hornby Castle Portal*, which formed part of the refurbishments of Hornby Castle in Yorkshire carried out by William, Lord Conyers (1468-1524), and the arch bears the name 'Conyers' below the family arms, a lavish heraldic display typical of the age. It is the largest of a series of imposing medieval stone doorways, arches and windows incorporated into the modern structure. They give the new fabric of the building a sense of age and permanence and also provide a link between the architectural framework and the Collection itself. All the ancient stonework was acquired by Burrell in 1953-4 from the vast collection formed by the legendary American newspaper proprietor William Randolph Hearst and its purchase shows the former's remarkable farsightedness. The large bronze nude statues by **Auguste Rodin** (1840-1917), entitled *The Age of Bronze* and *Eve after the Fall*, speak for Burrell's liking for 19th-century art.

7 The Hornby Castle Portal   *English, early 16th century*   *Sandstone, 6·86×2·29m (22½×7½ft)* *Formerly in the collection of William Randolph Hearst.*   *Reg. no. 44/100*

17

8 *The north-west corner of the gallery, with Egyptian artefacts seen against a woodland backdrop. Photograph by Alastair Hunter*

Through the Hornby Portal is the NORTH GALLERY and the beginning of the Collection proper. The north wall of the building is of glass, allowing an exciting interplay between the objects displayed within and the world outside. The works of art take on different qualities through the changes of natural light. In winter they can be starkly silhouetted against a bare landscape and lit by a strong, cold light or low winter sun; in the same season different impressions are imparted by the artificial lighting and the dramatic illumination of the trees and undergrowth. In the autumn they can borrow something of the mellowness and subdued colours of the woodland; in spring and summer the bluebells and foliage provide a backdrop setting echoed by the *verdure* tapestries displayed in the Hutton Castle rooms and Tapestry Gallery.

The North Gallery is, therefore, a veritable 'walk through the woods'. By following it the entire length of the building the visitor will pass through all the major areas of the Collection.

The first of these, which is entered from the Hornby Portal, comprises the **ANCIENT CIVILIZATIONS** of Egypt, Greece, Italy, Iraq, Iran and Turkey. This was the last section of the Collection to be formed by Sir William Burrell and the objects in it were mainly acquired in the late 1940s and early 1950s.

Artefacts from **Ancient Egypt** are exhibited in the first area of the North Gallery. The items displayed range from the Predynastic period (c.4000-3100 B.C.), to the times of Greek rule in Egypt (the Ptolemaic period, 332-30 B.C.).

In the showcase on the wall to the left is a series of *shawabtis* in limestone, alabaster and other materials, in addition to some small sculptors' models and miniature glass bottles. *Shawabti* figures were included in burials to act as substitutes for the deceased if they were called upon to serve in work gangs in the next world. They usually bear the owner's name. Another common type of grave good was the *stela*, a stone slab inscribed with the name of the deceased and requests for the supply of funerary offerings. The *stela* of Amenemhet, which dates from the early 18th Dynasty (c.1560-1450 B.C.), is displayed on the wall close to the *shawabtis*. In the corner next to these cases is a splendid head of a queen or goddess in basalt, dating from the late period (c.1085-332 B.C.), and opposite, towards the north-west angle of the gallery, a granite figure of

9 *Esmin* from Karnak. The two cases adjoining the column mainly contain vessels in alabaster, basalt, marble and other hard stones, chiefly of the Predynastic period.

Several of the large sculpture items are mounted on the free-

10 standing plinths; some represent deities, such as the *Sekhmet* on the stand facing the Courtyard, and the bronze statuette of *Osiris*, god of the Underworld; other are of mortals, including the granite relief of the pharaoh *Ramesses II* (1290-1224 B.C.) on the east wall. The quartzite statue of Ramesses' third son, the chief charioteer *Pa-*

9 Block Statue of Esmin   *Egyptian, 26th Dynasty (664-525 B.C.)*   *Granite, height 33·0cm (13in)*   *Reg. no. 13/233*

10 Head of Sekhmet   *Egyptian New Kingdom, 18th Dynasty Reign of Amenophis III (1402-1363 B.C.)*   *Granite, height 30·4cm (12in)*   *Reg. no. 13/181*

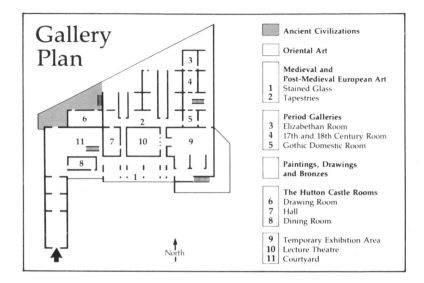

Gallery Plan

	Ancient Civilizations	
	Oriental Art	
	Medieval and	
	Post-Medieval European Art	
1	Stained Glass	
2	Tapestries	
	Period Galleries	
3	Elizabethan Room	
4	17th and 18th Century Room	
5	Gothic Domestic Room	
	Paintings, Drawings	
	and Bronzes	
	The Hutton Castle Rooms	
6	Drawing Room	
7	Hall	
8	Dining Room	
9	Temporary Exhibition Area	
10	Lecture Theatre	
11	Courtyard	

North

ra-her-wenem-ef, is interesting for costume details.

There are objects associated with tombs to the right of the entrance from the Courtyard. The painted limestone relief of a man offering a cup and a goose formed part of the mural decoration of a funerary chamber of the 6th Dynasty (*c*.2420-2250 B.C.), and from the Ptolemaic period comes the monumental head from a coffin lid.

The next section in the North Gallery is primarily devoted to **Greek and Roman** items. The earliest Greek pieces include an earthenware Mycenaean stem vase and a small terracotta chariot drawn by two horses, dating from *c*.1250-1200 B.C.. These are displayed in the large showcase in the centre but most of the artefacts in this case are of the 6th and 5th centuries B.C., regarded as the golden age of Greek art. There are some fine examples of vase-painting using both the black-figure and red-figure techniques in this case and on individual plinths. There are *amphora* (storage jars), oil jugs, *kraters* for mixing wine, scent bottles, a drinking horn known as a *rhyton* (in the form of a sheep's head) and two-handled shallow drinking cups, some of them decorated with scenes from classical mythology. The black-figure *amphora* nearest to the Egyptian area has fabulous and real creatures and masks. Some of the vases in the Collection have been attributed to individual

11 *The North Gallery looking east. Photograph by Keith Gibson*

painters. The red-figure *krater* in the central showcase is by a South Italian artist of the 4th century B.C. known as the **Sydney Painter**. The *lekythos*, or oil jug, in the same case is considered to be the work of the **Gela Painter**, who was active from *c.*508 to 485 B.C. in Gela, a town in Sicily founded by Greeks from Rhodes.

12

The same showcase contains several *helmets*, including a 6th-century bronze example, pierced with nail-holes for mounting as a votive offering in a temple after battle; the large *amphora* towards the end of this section has warriors wearing helmets of the same design. Several of the vases are from southern Italy, an area colonized by the Greeks in the 8th and 7th centuries B.C. Other cultures were established in Italy during ancient times. The **Etruscans** were noted for their bronze craftsmanship and the central showcase includes Etruscan helmets and household utensils. There is a fine *cista* (toilet-box) with incised decoration of combat.

The best known of the Italian cultures is that of **Rome** and a selection of its artefacts is distributed in the cases round the edge of this part of the gallery. On the south wall are glass vessels of various types, next to a fine fragment of a floor mosaic depicting a cockerel. The porphyry head of the god *Zeus* or *Poseidon*, a bronze bust of *Hermes* and a marble torso set on the three plinths in front of the glass wall all reveal the debt of ancient Rome to ancient Greece.

Beyond the Greek and Roman displays are several showcases containing objects from what is now **Iraq, Iran and eastern Turkey**. The earliest pieces are in the recessed case at the foot of the stairs to the Mezzanine and in the two small wall-cases behind the late 13th-century French limestone doorway. These artefacts are from **Mesopotamia**, the classical name for the district between the Tigris and Euphrates rivers, and they represent the various **Sumerian** cultures that flourished there from 5000 to 2000 B.C. The objects include *alabaster votive statuettes* which were placed in the sanctuary of a religious building to interecede with the deity, and tiny *seals* and *pendants* in the form of animals and birds.

Back through the 13th-century doorway, on the south wall is the fearsome, almost life-size terracotta *head of a lion* which probably came from a temple. It belongs to the **Isin-Larsa** civilization, one of the cultures that succeeded the Sumerian. Around 1800 B.C. the **Assyrians** established themselves in northern Iraq on the river Tigris. In the Neo-Assyrian period (*c.*1000-612 B.C.) they formed a powerful empire under a series of great rulers. Nearly every year their disciplined and organized forces fought campaigns to keep in

2   **13**   **14**

12 Lekythos   *Greek, Attic black figure, c.500 B.C.   Earthenware, height 25·0cm (9⁷⁄₈in)*   Reg. no. 19/95

13 Scribes Recording on Waxed Writing Boards   *Assyrian relief, period of Sennacherib-Ashurbanipal (704-627 B.C.), probably from the S.W. Palace of Kuyunjik (Nineveh), Iraq.   Alabaster, 18·2×15·0×1·5cm (7³⁄₈×5⁷⁄₈×⁵⁄₈in)   Reg. no. 28/33*

14 Bull's Head Cauldron Attachment   *Urartian, probably from Toprak Kale, Lake Van, Turkey,   7th century B.C.   Bronze, height 14·3cm (5⁵⁄₈in)   Reg. no. 33/212*

check the barbarians on the borders. These campaigns were commemorated on the alabaster reliefs which covered the walls of many rooms in the royal palaces at Nimrud and Nineveh. On the

13 fragments of *reliefs* which are displayed against the wall in front of the Mezzanine stairs are details of the campaigns, and of the weapons, dress and equipment of the soldiers. The reliefs date from the 9th to the 7th centuries B.C..

14 The small case next to the Mezzanine Stairs contains a fine *bull's head*, representing the kingdom of **Urartu**, which was contemporary with the Assyrian Empire. The metal workers of **Luristan** in the western part of modern Iran were famous for their craftsmanship in bronze, examples of which are displayed in the showcase next to the eastern entrance to the HUTTON CASTLE DRAWING ROOM.

15 The DRAWING ROOM is the largest of the three Hutton rooms and was Burrell's main display area for tapestries and stained glass. The first window from the left contains two 15th-century angels holding shields of arms from the chapel of the former Hospital of St John at Northampton, as well as several small English heraldic panels. In the two main lights of the centre window is a French

15 *The Hutton Castle Drawing Room from the west end.*

early 16th-century *Annunciation*, with small shields of arms and roundels above and below. The lights at the top contain a medley of 14th and 15th-century English glass. The chief elements of the right-hand window are the full-length figures of *St Peter* and an *archbishop-saint*, surmounted by two angels painted in East Anglia. At the top are figures of a female saint and a bearded donor. The ancient glass in the west window is confined to the three small lights and comprises two late 15th-century panels with the arms of Howard, Duke of Norfolk, and of the Vere Earls of Oxford, separated by a French roundel depicting the *Annunciation* and the cleric who was its donor.

Between the windows facing into the Courtyard are two early 16th-century **Franco-Flemish tapestries** from a set of the Labours of the Months, thought to be a product of the Tournai workshops of **16 Arnoult Poissonnier**. The first, for *January*, depicts a man, probably personifying the month, seated before a roaring fire being plied with food and drink whilst outside a primitive form of golf or hockey is in progress. The companion tapestry illustrates the activities associated with the month of *September*, with huntsmen setting ferrets to catch rabbits; in the background a peasant casts seed on a ploughed field. Two more Franco-Flemish hangings in this room belong to the type known as *millefleurs* because of their multi-flowered backgrounds. One of these shows *Johannes von Schleinitz*, Bishop of Naumburg (1422-34), and probably formed part of a series depicting bishops of this see woven in the period 1525-50. The second (viewed from the west door) depicts *Charity overcoming Envy* and almost certainly belonged to a large set depicting a series of battles between the Seven Cardinal Virtues and the Vices mounted on allegorical animals. Two of the remaining tapestries displayed at the west end of the room bear the arms of William III of Beaufort, his wife Eleanor of Comminges and their son Raymond, Vicomte de Turenne. They were almost certainly commissioned by William, who married Eleanor in 1349.

The other textiles in the Drawing Room consist of **Persian and Caucasian rugs and carpets** mainly of 19th-century date, and needlework and tapestry coverings on various chairs and settees. The **furniture coverings** are all English, of the period *c*.1690-*c*.1760, supplemented by several contemporary Netherlandish cushions. The **furniture** is chiefly oak and walnut, dating from the 17th century. Near the large Late Gothic stone fireplace and

17 chimneypiece is an unusual *clock* with wing pieces to allow wider oscillation of the pendulum. The movement is for a duration of 30 hours and the case is decorated in red lacquer with *chinoiserie* motifs.

16 Tapestry Depicting the Month of January   *Franco-Netherlandish, early 16th century   Wool, 271·7×320cm (107×126in)   Reg. no. 46/75*

17 Miniature Long-Case Clock *(detail of upper section)   English, inscribed 'Markwick Markham Perigal London', 18th century   Lacquered wooden case, 167·7×11·4cm (66×4½in)   Formerly at Cold Ashton Manor, Gloucestershire. Reg. no. 10/5*

On the tables and in the two wooden niches on the east wall is some interesting **medieval sculpture**, most of it late 15th or early 16th-century Netherlandish or German. The tall group of *St Anne holding the Virgin and the Child Christ* in front of the large tapestry on the east wall is a notable example of south German limewood carving.

After the Ancient Civilizations comes **ORIENTAL ART**. With 2000 items, this is numerically the largest section of the Collection. It is particularly strong in Chinese ceramics and bronzes, and is one of the most important collections in the British Isles in these fields. Precisely what sparked off Sir William Burrell's taste for Far Eastern art is unknown, but his interest was aroused at quite an early stage in his collecting career. By the early years of the 20th century he already owned Chinese ceramics and the Purchase Books record that he acquired in this area almost every year between 1911 and 1957. His most prolific period of activity was 1945-8 when he bought more than 120 pieces per year, including some of the best items in the Collection. Burrell had a particular liking for early ceramics, and also for bronzes.

There is a selection of Oriental ceramics and bronzes in the open area immediately beyond the Ancient Civilizations displays and the ORIENTAL DAYLIT GALLERY which runs north-south, contains showcases filled almost entirely with Chinese ceramics. On the right as you approach is a carpeted room with a low ceiling and a reduced level of lighting for the display of **Japanese prints**. This small group of thirty 18th and 19th-century woodblock prints has examples of most of the leading artists of the time, including **Katsushika Hokusai** (1760-1849) and **Kitagawa Utamaro** (1750-1806). The beautiful print at the left end of the south wall of an *Old Fisherman* smoking his pipe is considered to be a self-portrait of Hokusai. One of the prints by Utamaro depicts a *Seated Courtesan*; this and several other prints show how popular the world of courtesans and geishas was with the artists. Other common themes were taken from Japanese theatre (as in the fine Hokusai print of the *Segawa* actor), popular literature and semi-religious and legendary figures. One of the most dramatic of the Burrell prints in the last category is that of *Shōki the Demon Queller* by **Utagawa Kunisada** (1786-1865). Equally awe-inspiring but very different in style is the *Shōki* by **Utagawa Toyoharu** (1735-1814).

All of the prints displayed on the east wall, in addition to the Hokusai *Old Fisherman* mentioned above, are *surimono*, small prints made for special occasions such as marriage, a birthday or the New

18

18 Kitagawa Utamaro (1750-1806): *Seated Courtesan   Japanese, c.1795-7 Woodblock print on paper, 38·1×25·4cm (15×10in).   Reg. no. 37/7*

Year. These are of particularly high quality, with very delicate printing and the use of various metal dusts. All of the *surimono* exhibited here include poems in the design. One of these is the very colourful print of the *Female Warrior Tomoe Gozen* by **Aiogaoka Hokkei** (1780-1850). In a fight with a man wielding a pine trunk, this heroine of medieval legend wrested the branch from her assailant and broke it in splinters. A wide variety of styles is exhibited in these prints, but all display that calligraphic sensitivity so characteristic of Japanese art.

In the space outside the Japanese Prints Room are some of the most important and attractive of the **Chinese Ceramics and Bronzes**, in addition to a few sculptures and a fine 16th-century *cloisonné* enamelled dish. The earliest items are the large bronze *lian*, or cylindrical box with ring handles and three legs in human form, the earthenware lead-glazed *watchdog* and the model of a *storehouse*, all of which date from the Han Dynasty (206 B.C.- A.D. 220); the last two were made specifically for burial with the dead. The watchdog in his carefully detailed harness was intended to protect his master in the next world. The storehouse, complete with figures carrying sacks, is very important for the information it provides about early Chinese architecture. Ceramic grave goods reached a peak of magnificence during the Tang Dynasty (A.D. 618-907) with the splendid horses and camels and elegantly dressed figures. An example of each of these can be seen in this area, all made with the *sancai* or three-colour glaze of green, amber and cream. The trappings of the horse reflect Persian Sassanian influence and the male attendant figure in the same showcase wears Central Asian dress. The face and neck of this attendant are unglazed and painted with unfired pigments, a characteristic treatment for human or semi-human figures in this period. It also appears on the pair of figures with fierce expressions standing at the entrance to the Oriental Daylit Gallery, where they perform something like their original function as guardians of tombs against evil spirits. They are representatives of the spirit world in exaggerated human form and are known as *fangxiang* figures.

The largest showcase in this part of the North Gallery contains some very fine Chinese porcelains from the Yuan and early Ming Dynasties, with underglaze cobalt blue and copper-red decoration. These underglazes were introduced in the 14th century by the potters of Jingdezhen in the province of Jiangxi: many of the wares, such as the large dish and tankard, were made for the Near Eastern market and are based on designs from this region. The splendid copper-red *ewer* derives its shape from a Near Eastern metalwork vessel and includes decorative motifs of Near Eastern origin, although the latter are combined with Chinese traditional designs.

19   Very different from the Ming porcelains are the monumental seated figures near the North Wall of a *Lohan* (disciple of Buddha), dated 1484, and of an official, which was made in 1609. Both are stoneware with overglaze enamel decoration in colours similar to that of the nearby Tang pieces. An excellent vista can be obtained from the Lohan looking down the Oriental Daylit Gallery and through to the stained glass on the south side of the building.

19 Figure of a Lohan   *Chinese, Ming Dynasty, inscribed 20th year of Chenghua (A.D. 1484)   Stoneware with polychrome on biscuit glaze and traces of gilding, 126·8×66·7×43·2cm (50in×26½in×17in)   Reg. no. 38/419*

Gallery Plan

Ancient Civilizations

Oriental Art

Medieval and
Post-Medieval European Art
1 Stained Glass
2 Tapestries

Period Galleries
3 Elizabethan Room
4 17th and 18th Century Room
5 Gothic Domestic Room

Paintings, Drawings
and Bronzes

The Hutton Castle Rooms
6 Drawing Room
7 Hall
8 Dining Room

9 Temporary Exhibition Area
10 Lecture Theatre
11 Courtyard

North

20   Viewing of the **Chinese ceramics** in the ORIENTAL DAYLIT GALLERY is best begun at the far end with some painted *earthenware urns*. They are associated with the Neolithic Yangshao culture and date from the third millenium B.C. The larger pair of recessed showcases also contain some attractive Han Dynasty *grave goods*, including a pair of owls and two cockerels, as well as a pair of guardian figures from the Six Dynasties period. More ceramic models from tombs, this time of the Tang Dynasty period, are displayed in the two projecting cases below the Mezzanine. The vivid and dramatic poses of the acrobat and the horse fiercely pawing the ground can be contrasted with the gentler pursuits of music-making and with the set of five very slender servants carrying various objects. Tang ceramics also fill the double-sided showcase on the east side of the Gallery. The case opposite contains the very beautiful *ding* wares of the Song Dynasty (A.D. 960-1279). The earliest of these vessels have incised designs and the later have moulded decorations. Both incised and moulded patterns can be seen on the *ginghai* wares (porcelain with a slightly bluish glaze) dating from the Yuan Dynasty (A.D. 1260-1368). In the next (recessed) case on the east side are some of the extremely beautiful

21   *black wares* from Henan province; also a series of tea bowls demonstrating the range of decorative motifs used on black glazes:

20 *The Oriental Daylit Gallery on a winter evening. Photograph by Alastair Hunter*

21 Three Tea Bowls *(1) North Chinese, Northern Song-Jin Dynasty, 12th-13th century* A.D. *Stoneware, slipped and glazed with splash decoration, 4·5×12·4cm (1³/₄×4⁷/₈in)* Reg. no. 38/347
(2) North Chinese, Henan Province, Jin Dynasty 12th-13th century A.D. *Stoneware, slipped and glazed with speckled effect, 5·4×12·7cm (2¹/₄×5in)* Reg. no. 38/348
(3) Chinese, Fujian Province, Southern Song Dynasty, 12-13th century A.D. *Jian ware, stoneware with viscous black blaze with 'hare's fur' effect, 5·1×12·1cm (2×4³/₄in)* Reg. no. 38/359

speckled, splashed, streaked and those based on paper-cuts. All these date from the 12th to the 14th centuries A.D. A particularly attractive piece in the companion showcase on the west side is the model of a *recumbent tiger*, made during the Song Dynasty.

Amongst the most popular of Chinese ceramics is the green-glazed stoneware known as *celadon*, examples of which can be seen in one of the two projecting showcases. The ware was first made in the 9th century A.D., but it was not fully established until the following century and reached its peak during the Northern Song Dynasty (A.D. 960-1126). From this time celadon wares have been much admired in China and are still made there today. Opposite the celadons are porcelains with underglaze cobalt blue decoration, from the Ming and Qing Dynasties. Near Eastern shapes and motifs are well to the fore on several of the vessels, including the *meiping* vase with Arabic inscriptions. Many of the later blue and white wares have scenes or figures. That on the large *rouleau* vase depicts the Emperor on his pleasure barge. Not only blue and white porcelains were produced during the Ming and Qing Dynasties, as is shown by the displays in the last pair of showcases in the Oriental Daylit Gallery. One contains a selection of the *monochrome* (or single glaze) *porcelains* in various colours, including copper-red, ox-blood, peach-bloom and yellow (the Imperial colour). The peach-bloom vase and the beehive-shaped water pot were made for a scholar's table. In the case on the opposite wall are other vessels concerned with writing, including a charming *water pot* in the shape of a tree shrew and a *brush rest*; the latter is embellished in enamels on biscuit porcelain. During the 16th century overglaze enamel decoration became popular in China. Sir William Burrell particularly liked the wares with *famille verte* enamels and there are a large number in the Collection. A representative group is exhibited here.

The *conical bowl* in one of the pair of small showcases at the end of the Gallery is amongst the rarest pieces in the entire Collection. It is an example of a particular Korean variant of the celadon wares and is painted with copper-red decoration under the celadon glaze. This bowl dates from the Koryo Dynasty (12th and 13th centuries A.D.).

22 *Four Turkish prayer rugs, 17th and 18th centuries* A.D. *Photograph by Keith Gibson*

On the east side of the Daylit Gallery is a room devoted almost entirely to **Islamic Prayer Rugs**. These are all quite small, usually less than two metres in length, and although they are displayed as wall-hangings they were – and still are – used in the Muslim world to cover the floors of mosques and by the devout to kneel on and face Mecca during the required periods of daily prayer. The prayer rugs in the Collection come from the Anatolian heartland of
22 Turkey, Persia (Iran) and the Caucasus (present-day southern

USSR) and mainly date between the 17th and 19th centuries. Though varying from region to region, most of the rugs have in common a representation of the *mihrab*, the prayer niche in a mosque wall which indicates the direction of Mecca. The earliest of the Islamic carpets in the Collection is the *fragment* displayed in one of the recessed showcases. This is a piece of the border from one of two carpets formerly in the mosque of Ardabil in Persia, of which various segments are scattered in museums around the world. These carpets are dated by inscription to the Muslim year 946 (A.D. 1539-40) and were made for the shrine of Sheikh Safi, the founder of the Safavid Dynasty. In the same case is a fragment of another Persian carpet, of the 18th century, and a very fine section from the border of an *Indian animal carpet*. The latter is very finely woven with fishes and the heads of horses, lions and oxen in a lattice-work of plant sprays. A larger section of an Indian animal carpet can be seen in the South Gallery (see p.69). In the other showcase is a selection from the small group of **Coptic textiles** in the Burrell Collection. They were found in Egyptian burials of the 4th-9th centuries A.D. and the dry climate and sand account for their good state of preservation. In this period Egypt was predominantly Christian (hence the name Coptic textiles, after the Coptic Church of Egypt), but the debt to the heritage of ancient Greece is apparent in some of the designs, notably that of two winged figures on one of the fragments.

The next section of the North Gallery is concerned with decorative arts from the **MIDDLE AGES AND NORTHERN RENAISSANCE**. The art of the period *c.*1300-1530 was always Sir William Burrell's first love, as is apparent from the contents of the reconstructed rooms from Hutton Castle.

Burrell's interest in the Middle Ages was aroused at an early age and continued to the end of his life. It may be significant that his schooldays were spent in St Andrews, where there are evocative remains of important medieval buildings; as a young man he was also well-acquainted with the medieval castles in the East Neuk of Fife. By the turn of the century he had purchased a representative range of medieval artefacts, including tapestries, items for ecclesiastical and domestic use, and sculptures in wood, alabaster and ivory.

Even within the confines of the medieval period Burrell had his likes and dislikes; it was only with considerable difficulty, for instance, that he could be persuaded to buy pieces earlier than the 14th century. It is somewhat ironic, therefore, that some of the most highly valued medieval items in the entire Collection date from before 1300. A number of these pieces are on display in the first room on the right after the Oriental section. This room is fronted by the large free-standing *English arch* of *c*.1200, carved with a profusion of rosettes and geometric shapes.

The two recessed showcases contain a selection of small medieval objects – ivories, Limoges enamels and bronzes dated from the 12th to the 14th centuries. In the left-hand case pride of place perhaps goes to the *Temple Pyx*, a small bronze-gilt group of three sleeping knights almost certainly representing the soldiers at the Holy Sepulchre and originally forming part of a 12th-century English **23** shrine or reliquary. The *ivory draughtsman* is of the same epoch.

23 Draughtsman   *German, late 12th century   Ivory, diameter 5·7cm (2⅕ in)*
Reg. no. 21/2

Other particularly noteworthy pieces include the enamelled reliquary *châsse*, or casket, made at Limoges, in *c*.1200-10, on which is depicted the martyrdom of Thomas à Becket; also, in the right-hand case, an early 14th-century German bronze *aquamanile* in the form of a lion from Brilon in Westphalia. Aquamaniles, as the Latin name suggests, held water and were frequently used in church services, but as this example bears Hebrew inscriptions they were not exclusively confined to Christian use.

Most of the medieval pieces in the Collection come from northern Europe, but against the south wall of this room is a group of large Spanish objects. The effigy on the tomb, resplendent in chain mail and an elaborately decorated surcoat, represents *Don Ramon Peralta de Espès* (d.1348), Captain-General of the armies of the kingdom of nragon and Grand-Admiral of Aragon and Sicily. This monument, which retains much of its original painted decoration, comes from the monastery of Santa Maria de Obarra at Calvera near Huesca in northern Spain. The painted wooden figures of the *Virgin* and *St John* above the tomb are probably from the same region but are somewhat earlier, dating from the late 13th century. They originally formed part of a Crucifixion group.

24 Virgin and Child   *English, Nottingham, late 14th century   Alabaster, height 46·3cm (22½in)   Reg. no. 1/19*

25 Sallet   *South German, Augsburg, c.1480   Steel, 22·8×37·4×22·2cm (9×14¾×8¾in) Formerly in the collection of Morgan S. Williams   Reg. no. 2/10*

    The other large items in the room are worth a close study.

24 Between the two recessed showcases is a highly important *Virgin and Child* in alabaster and, on the opposite wall, the *Bury Chest* is one of a very rare group of English oak coffers with painted heraldic decoration. It comes from the Chancery Court of the Palatinate of Durham and was made during Richard de Bury's reign as Bishop of Durham (1334-45). He was much employed in the service of the English crown and was noted for his fine library, splendid retinue and sumptuous living.

    The vestment in the freestanding showcase is a *dalmatic*, which was worn by deacons at Mass. It has two wide strips known as orphreys embroidered with scenes from the early life of the Virgin and her parents Joachim and Anne. These scenes are of great charm, none more so than that of the Virgin taking her first steps with the aid of a wooden baby-walker, watched anxiously by her mother and father. The dalmatic is Italian, and the orphreys are an example of English needlework known as *opus anglicanum*, which was justly admired throughout western Christendom. The vestment forms part of a set said to have belonged before the Reformation to the Cistercian abbey of Whalley in Lancashire.

    In the area in front of the glass north wall are some notable works of **medieval sculpture**. The small-scale delicacy of the boxwood *Virgin and Child* of c.1325-50 may be contrasted with the more monumental treatment in limestone of the same subject and of a female saint. Together with the *Head of the Virgin* they reveal the quality of French Gothic sculpture of the period 1250-1350. The large *Virgin and Child* statuette in front of one of the columns was originally painted and retains two of the glass inserts imitating jewels in the hem of her robe.

Guarding the entrance to the EUROPEAN DAYLIT GALLERY are two early 16th-century *South German armours*. The simplicity and functional nature of that on the right, made for the battlefield, is in contrast with the elaborate etched decoration of its companion, designed for ceremonial or tournament use. The latter is a composite, made up of elements from various suits; the most important sections were made by a leading armourer, **Michael Witz** of Innsbruck, for the Emperor Ferdinand I (1503-64). The martial theme continues in the first six cases in the European Daylit Gallery, which contain a selection of armours and weapons, including a series of swords dating from *c*.1200 to the early 16th-century. The hilt of the *Coventry Civic Sword* is the most important historically and the etched decoration on the Milanese half armour of *c*.1570 is particularly fine. The Augsburg *sallet* is probably the most outstanding of the helmets. The only firearm in the Collection is the Scottish *pistol* dated 1649.

26 Tyg (large drinking vessel)   *English, Staffordshire, c.1675   Earthenware, height 16·5cm (6½in)   Reg. no. 39/92*

The remainder of the European Daylit Gallery beyond the pair of limestone windows is devoted to **European decorative arts** from the 14th to the 18th centuries. The Burrell Collection is not generally known for its European *ceramics*, but there are some very fine examples of tin-glazed earthenware, particularly those made in Valencia, Spain, in the period *c*.1430-1550. The eye-catching gold-lustre decoration of these dishes is very different from the English *slipware* (a style of decorating the earthenware with a diluted clay of a different colour) made in Staffordshire during the late 17th and early 18th centuries. Two of the slipware pieces are 'signed' by

26   **Thomas Toft**, one of the leading potters of the period. The German stoneware jugs and tankards are notable for their heraldic decoration. Heraldry also plays its part in the decoration of some of the large *pewter plates*, or chargers, which have some of the naivety and simplicity of their slipware counterparts. One dated 1677 commemorates the reconstruction of the City of London following the Great Fire of 1666 by a phoenix rising from the flames and a bust of King Charles II.

The delicacy of the *table glass* and *silverware* contrasts strongly with the vigour of the pewter and pottery. The outstanding craftsmanship of the Dutch engravers of the 18th century is seen in the Dutch, English and German wine glasses and goblets. Two showcases contain *glassware*, unengraved except for a large English goblet commemorating the battle of Trafalgar in 1805. This is seen to best advantage from the Needlework Room (see pp.78-81).

The Collection contains nearly 300 silver items, mostly English. The pieces displayed in the eight showcases at the end of the European Daylit Gallery are of 17th and 18th-century date and include tankards and other drinking vessels, spoons, salvers, plates and candlesticks. There is a fine *toilet set* in its original container made for the Hurst family of Lincolnshire. Burrell's taste is evident in the comparatively simple decoration of the silver; for him the work of the Huguenot (French Protestant) goldsmiths who settled in England in the late 18th century was too elaborate. There is, however, one outstanding example of Huguenot engraved silver in the Collection, the *salver* made for the Earl of Halifax. Above it is another interesting historical item, a silver-mounted *coconut cup* dated 1662 carved with scenes illustrating the escape of King Charles II after the battle of Worcester.

27   In the European Daylit Gallery, a pair of *limestone windows* provide an attractive framework for a view into the MEDIEVAL ROOMS which flank this space. One of these rooms has already been visited and the second is reached by returning up the Daylit

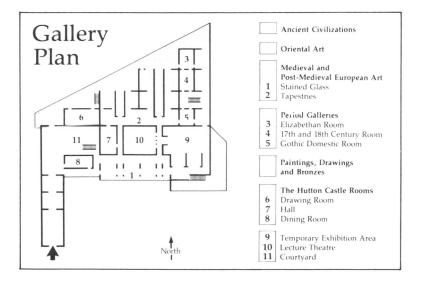

Gallery Plan

	Ancient Civilizations
	Oriental Art

Medieval and Post-Medieval European Art
1 Stained Glass
2 Tapestries

Period Galleries
3 Elizabethan Room
4 17th and 18th Century Room
5 Gothic Domestic Room

Paintings, Drawings and Bronzes

The Hutton Castle Rooms
6 Drawing Room
7 Hall
8 Dining Room

9 Temporary Exhibition Area
10 Lecture Theatre
11 Courtyard

North

27 Window in the European Daylit Gallery *French, late 15th early-16th centuries Limestone, height 289·5cm. (9ft 6in) Formerly in the collection of William Randolph Hearst. Reg. no. 44/91*

28 Choir Stalls   *French, c.1450-1500   Oak, 299·7×97·0×76·2cm (9ft 10in×7ft 5in×2ft 6in)   Formerly in the collection of William Randolph Hearst.   Reg. no. 14/5*

Gallery towards the glass north wall, turning right and right again through the large free-standing *sandstone arch* which forms the entrance. The high-relief carved decoration on this portal includes some amusing scenes of wrestling monkeys, birds, a cat, thistles and youths picking acorns. The presence of palm trees indicates that the arch must come from a Mediterranean country, probably Spain or Portugal. It dates from the early 16th century.

The second MEDIEVAL ROOM is devoted almost entirely to objects and furnishings used in the Church during the Middle Ages. The most complete item of furniture is the set of canopied **28** *choir stalls* with three *misericords*, hinged seats with projecting ledges on the underside which when tipped up provided a support for the clergy during the lengthy services. These ledges allowed the medieval carver to give full rein to his creative imagination. The six misericord seats mounted on the east wall demonstrate the wide range of designs used: animals, monsters, human figures and heads, and Noah's Ark.

One of the richly-embellished *stall-ends* on the south wall depicts a prophet and angels and is of late 15th-century southern Netherlandish origin. The presence of St Quirinus, whose shrine was at Neuss in the Lower Rhineland, suggests that the companion stall-end comes from this region. It may be the work of a sculptor named **Heinrich Bernts** (d.1509).

The English late medieval wood-carver was as uninhibited as his continental counterpart. Appropriately, angels were a common subject in the decoration of English church roofs and there is a set of four above the six misericords on the east wall. They are playing a variety of musical instruments, including the clarion, tabor and shawm and date from the late 15th or early 16th century.

Tombs and monuments formed a major elements in the furnishings of medieval churches. The three angels holding shields and enclosed within niches come from one side of a late 15th-century *alabaster tomb chest* of a type widely distributed in England. Tombs were not always made of stone and alabaster; frequently the deceased was commemorated by a monumental brass set into a slab in the floor. There are three *brasses* in the two recessed showcases in this room, the most impressive of which commemorates the historian and mapmaker John Speed (1542-1629). The majority of the objects in these two showcases formed part of **altar furnishings** or were used in church services. They include large brass altar *candlesticks*, altar and processional *crosses* (one of which is a very rare example in rock crystal, dating from the 13th century), *chrismatories* used to contain the holy oils for Baptism, Confirmation and Extreme Unction and receptacles for the Sacramental bread (the Host) known as *pyxes* or *monstrances*. The *chalice* was the most elaborate of the liturgical vessels; one of those displayed here is made of silver, partly gilt, with translucent enamelling, and most unusually has the embossed figures of the donors, George and Margaret Sperling, kneeling before the Virgin and Child. It was made in northern Germany in the late 14th or early 15th century. In the centre of the room is an impressive English *chasuble* and, on the north wall, two very important *tapestry fragments*, which are related to the famous Apocalypse series at Angers, France.

29 Burgundian Altarpiece   *French, c.1450-1500   Painted limestone, 86·3×177·8cm (1ft 10in×5ft 10in)   Reg. no. 44/36*

30 Figure of Christ   *South Netherlandish, late 15th century   Painted oak, height 51·4cm (20¼in)   Reg. no. 50/21*

The ecclesiastical theme continues through the arch and back into the North Gallery, where there is a major display of retables or **altarpieces**, the dominant sculptural form of the 15th and early 16th centuries. The *Burgundian altarpiece* has been placed on an imitation altar to give the impression of the original setting of such retables. The figures on it bear witness to the long-lived influence of Claus Sluter, the Netherlandish-born carver who in the years around 1400 established a distinctive school of sculpture in Burgundy. As can be observed from the examples shown here, the design of retables varied considerably in northern Europe. The most elaborate and attractive were the limewood altarpieces of southern Germany and those from the Tyrol, which were made of pine. Although there is no complete altarpiece from these regions in the Collection, it does include various components from them, such as the large early 16th-century *Lamentation over the dead Christ* which almost certainly formed the centrepiece of a retable from the Augsburg area. Painted altarpieces continued to be made in Germany well into the 1520s, but from the 1490s an alternative appeared in the form of the monochrome, or unpainted retable, which enabled the sculptor to carve very fine details; the limewood *Nativity* from the wing of a Franconian altarpiece of *c*.1500 is a good example of this. Late medieval altarpieces in England usually consisted of a row of alabaster panels depicting scenes from the life of Christ and/or the Virgin, and of individual saints, enclosed

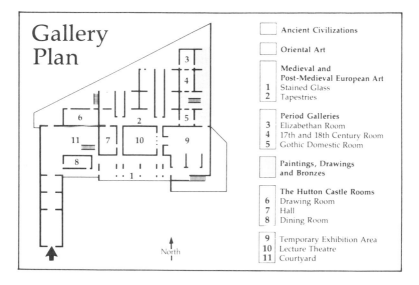

within a wooden framework. The panels displayed in the long case on the south wall come from various dismembered altarpieces. The English alabaster carvers also made individual cult images, such as the majestic *Holy Trinity* of 1375-85, set high on the wall over the Burgundian altarpiece. Alabaster was also used, indeed more proficiently, by sculptors in France, Germany and the Netherlands. The small *Pietà* in front of the Burgundian altarpiece can be attributed to the workshop of the **Rimini Master**, a highly accomplished artist who seems to have settled in the Middle Rhine area of Germany between *c*.1420 and 1430. The *Virgin and Child* set against the glass wall is a fine example of late 15th-century Netherlandish alabaster work. This piece is around the corner from the *Lamentation* sculpture and the tour now continues towards the far (east) wall. In front of the column in the middle of this space is a monumental limestone figure of *St Margaret of Antioch*; the delineation of the brocading on her dress and the hem decoration are characteristic of early 16th-century French sculpture. In the case on the east wall is a series of small late medieval wooden sculptures from Germany, Austria and the Netherlands. Some are individual devotional statuettes, such as the attractive painted and gilded *Virgin and Child* from Malines near Brussels. Others, like the *Figure*
30 *of Christ*, come from altarpieces. This originally formed the centrepiece of a Flagellation scene on a retable devoted to the Passion of Christ.

It is in this corner of the gallery that the earliest paintings in the Collection are displayed.

PAINTINGS were among the first works of art that Sir William Burrell acquired. He was already buying pictures in his teens and he was still amassing them two years before his death. His first taste was for 18th-century British portraiture, but before 1900 he had turned his attention to the Hague and Barbizon Schools and the contemporary 'Glasgow Boys'. Burrell's preferences in paintings were very strongly influenced by the art dealer Alexander Reid, who opened a gallery in Glasgow in 1889. Up to the 1920's Burrell bought consistently from him and it was Reid who pointed him in the direction of artists such as Boudin, Degas and Manet.

The real strength of the pictures collection lies in the French 19th-century schools, but there are also some fine earlier works, as can be readily observed from the row of 15th and 16th-century panel paintings on the north wall facing the woodlands. In the centre is *The Stag Hunt* by **Lucas Cranach the Elder** (1472-1553), which has been placed in this position as part of the interplay between art and nature throughout the North Gallery: the deer in the picture are sometimes mirrored by real deer in the woods outside. *The Stag Hunt* depicts an actual event, and amongst the figures in the foreground is the Holy Roman Emperor, Maximilian I (d.1529). Other notable paintings on this wall are another picture by

31 Cranach, *Cupid the Honey Thief complaining to Venus*, dated 1545, and two works by **Hans Memling** (c.1433-94), an exquisite *Annunciation* and *The Flight into Egypt*.

Sir William Burrell was a northerner by temperament and upbringing and he did not care overmuch for Italian art. It is somewhat ironic, therefore, that amongst the treasures of the Collection should be the **Florentine School** *Judgement of Paris*, and the *Virgin and Child* by the Venetian artist **Giovanni Bellini** (active c.1459-1516). The latter is accompanied by another fine work of contemporary Italian Renaissance sculpture, a marble bust of a boy which is possibly the work of the Florentine sculptor **Benedetto da Maiano** (1422-97).

From the Bellini the tour proceeds down the east side of the gallery, into the rooms devoted entirely to paintings, prints and drawings. The first two spaces contain **FRENCH PAINTINGS**; such is the strength of the Collection in this field that most of the major French artists from **Théodore Géricault** (1791-1824) to **Paul Cézanne** (1839-1906) are represented. In the first of the galleries, as well as pictures by **Antoine le Nain** (1588-1648) and **Jean-Baptiste Chardin** (1699-1779), there are also works by the leading Romantic

31 Lucas Cranach the Elder: *Cupid the Honey Thief Complaining to Venus, signed with the winged serpent device and dated 1545   Oil on panel, 51·5×36·2cm (20¼×14¼ in)   Formerly in the collection of Sir Thomas Gibson Carmichael, Bart. Reg. no. 35/74*

artists, notably **Géricault** and **Eugène Delacroix** (1798-1863). The lively and dramatic approach of such artists is well to the fore in their studies of horses and especially in *The Trumpeter of the Lancers of the Guard*. In the free use of paint and compositional values these paintings are a world far removed from the stillness and precision of *The Dog* by **Jean-Baptiste Oudry** (1686-1755). The frame of this striking picture disguises to some extent its original function, which was to act as a draught-excluder in a fireplace during the summer months. The background and perspective are designed to give the impression that the animal is standing in the fireplace.

32

32 Théodore Géricault: *The Trumpeter of the Lancers of the Guard, c.1812-15.*
Oil on canvas, 40·6×33·0cm (16×13in)   Reg. no. 35/270

Thomas Couture's austere *Le Conventionnel* of *c*.1848 retains many
of the traditional values challenged later in the century by other
artists represented in this room. Their canvases were a reaction to
the Neoclassical style, characterized by monumental paintings
depicting historical or mythological scenes, and favoured by the
French artistic establishment.

More and more painters considered this official art to be arid and irrelevant and sought after a freer technique and a subject-matter drawn from daily life. *The Charity of a Beggar at Ornans* painted in 1868 by **Gustave Courbet** (1819-77) was considered shocking because of its portrayal of the harsh realities of life for the poor as much as for the artist's crude handling of paint. *The Portrait of Mlle. Aubé de la Holde*, on the other hand, shows that Courbet was occasionally capable of tempering his radicalism sufficiently to depict young and wealthy Parisian ladies for financial gain.

Honoré Daumier (1808-79) is best known for his political and social caricatures which appeared in various journals, but canvases such as *The Heavy Burden*, reveal that he had a similar outlook on life to Courbet. Burrell liked Daumier's work and there are no fewer than nine oil paintings and nine watercolours and drawings of his in the Collection. It is possible that Burrell may have seen something of himself in *The Print Collector*, Daumier's study of a gentleman-connoisseur inspecting prospective purchases.

33

The other works hanging in this room are by the **Barbizon School**, a group of landscape artists who frequented Barbizon, near Paris. The images of peasants by **Jean François Millet** (1814-75) express the nobility as well as the drudgery of agricultural labour, whereas **Jean-Baptiste Corot** (1796-1875) and **Charles François Daubigny** (1817-79) painted the countryside as they saw it and not as the idealized pastoral idyll favoured by previous generations of painters.

33 Honoré Daumier: *The Print Collector, c.1860-63*   *Oil on canvas, 35·5×25·4cm (14×10in)*   *Reg. no. 35/210*

34 Eugène Boudin: *The Jetty at Trouville, signed and dated 1869*   *Oil on canvas 64·8×92·7cm (25½×36½in)*   *Reg. no. 35/43*

35   The second room of French paintings is devoted to the
Impressionists, and the brightness and immediacy of their pictures
make the works of the Barbizon School and other artists displayed
in the previous room seem sombre. The Impressionists brought
about the greatest artistic revolution of the 19th century, with their
attempts at capturing the transitory nature of movement and light
by rapid, vivid handling of paint. Their origins can be traced back to
the middle of the century through the Barbizon School and artists
such as **Johan Barthold Jongkind** (1819-91). His *Fabrique de Cuirs
Forts* deliberately turns its back on formal academic painting by its
depiction of a scene as everyday as the demolition of a factory in
Paris.

35 *The French Painting Gallery containing works by Boudin and Degas. Photograph by
Keith Gibson*

    Eugène Boudin (1824-98) spent most of his life painting along the
coast of his native Normandy. In his choice of subjects, in particular
of outdoor subjects, he was a major influence on several of the
Impressionist artists. Trouville, at the mouth of the Seine, was a
34 fashionable resort at the time, but in his paintings of it, *The Jetty at
Trouville* and *The Empress Eugénie on the Beach at Trouville*, he
concentrates on the atmospheric effects of sea and sky, rather than
on the fashionable company. Sir William Burrell appreciated
Boudin very much and there are eleven works by him in the

Collection. He also admired **Edouard Manet** (1832-83) who, although generally regarded as the leader of the Impressionists, was not in sympathy with all their aims. One of the forums for discussion by artists and writers of this period was the Parisian café, which also provided the painters with plentiful subject-matter. Manet's vision of it is seen in the *Café, Place du Théâtre Français* and *Women Drinking Beer*. Manet also painted some delightful still-lifes. The broad and free application of brush strokes in his *Roses in a Champagne Glass* is in contrast to the dry and precise treatment of the same subject in *Spring Flowers* by **Henri Fantin-Latour** (1836-1904). Fantin-Latour, although a contemporary of the Impressionists, held much more traditional views on art.

The second gallery is dominated by **Edgar Degas** (1834-1917), with the entire west wall occupied by six of his major paintings and pastels, less than a third of the total of 22 of his works in the Collection. Burrell liked Degas' pictures very much and in one letter expressed his regret that he had never met the artist. These six pictures show the extent to which the worlds of ballet and horse racing provided Degas' source material; half of his 2000 surviving works are devoted to ballet subjects. Degas was not especially interested in dancing and racing for their own sake; rather he was fascinated by the shapes and movements created by such activities.

36 Even the *Woman Looking Through Field Glasses* (1865) is a racing subject, for the picture is a study for a figure in a racecourse scene. Of the three ballet pictures usually exhibited here, only *The Rehearsal* (1874) is in oils; the other two, including *Dancers in a Box*, are in pastel. The largest picture by Degas in this room is neither a ballet nor horse racing subject but a portrait of the novelist and critic *Edmond Duranty* (1879). The artist was much influenced by Duranty's views on realism, which is reflected by the depiction of the man of letters in his study, surrounded by the tools of his trade.

Burrell does not appear to have liked full-blown Impressionism and there are only comparatively minor works by **Renoir** and **Pissarro** in the Collection and none at all by Monet. The only painting he owned which comes into this category at all is *The Bell-Tower, Noisy-le-Roi; Autumn* by **Alfred Sisley** (1839-99). Given Burrell's conservative tastes, it is all the more surprising to see as avant-garde a work of Post-Impressionism as **Cézanne's** *Le Château de Médan* in the Collection. This is one of a number of Burrell's paintings which have an interesting history. It depicts land belonging to the novelist Emile Zola and the picture was owned for a time by **Gauguin**, who described it in glowing terms in one of his letters. Gauguin was another artist who had a limited appeal for

36 Edgar Degas: *Woman Looking Through Field Glasses, c.*1865 *Oil on paper on canvas, 30·4×19·0cm (12 in×7½ in) Reg. no. 35/239*

Burrell. The sole example of his work in the Collection is the chalk drawing *The Breton Girl*, which can normally be seen in the next room on the tour, THE PRINTS AND DRAWINGS GALLERY. Owing to the damage drawings and watercolours can suffer through prolonged exposure even to subdued light, the works in this room will be changed quite frequently. This does not apply so much to the woodcuts by **Albrecht Dürer** (1471-1528) and **Lucas Cranach the Elder**, nor to the series of small etchings by **Rembrandt**.

The drawings and watercolours on the walls in the centre of the Prints and Drawings Gallery are all of the French School. They range from the delicate pencil portrait by **Ingres** (1780-1887) of *Tylman Suys*, the only Neoclassical work in the entire Collection, to Gauguin's *Breton Girl*. Other artists represented include Bonvin, Corot, Daumier, Degas, Manet and Millet. **Daumier's** *Bons Confrères*, a biting satire on the French legal system, should not be missed: two lawyers are greeting each other, oblivious to the grief of the woman emerging from the lawcourts in the background. The most haunting of **Millet's** pictures is *Winter, The Plain of Chailly*, a harsh and bleak landscape evocative of some of the novels of Emile Zola.

37 Joseph Crawhall: *The Flower Shop, c.*1890-1905   *Gouache on linen,*
27·4×34·3cm (10¾×13½ in)   Reg. no. 35/117

37   **Joseph Crawhall** (1861-1913) was one of the few contemporary artists patronized by Sir William Burrell, and there are more works (132) by him in the Collection than by any other artist. Burrell knew Crawhall well when the artist was a member of the 'Glasgow Boys' group at the end of the 19th century and he admired his technical mastery. If his ladies in governess carts and riding bicycles remind us of a lost Edwardian world, his portrayals of animals and birds often reveal a droll sense of humour and acute observation of nature.

On the east wall are some watercolours by **Johannes Bosboom** (1817-91), a Dutch contemporary of the French artists displayed in the room. In subject-matter, e.g. church interiors, he looked back to the great 17th-century masters of his native country, although his style was very different. The fluid washes and calligraphic lines were to prove very influential on the **Hague School**, whose works are hung in the third Painting Gallery.

The artists of this group, established at The Hague by 1870, were popular with Scottish, particularly Glasgow, collectors, and several of the dealers there stocked their works. In common with the Barbizon School and Impressionist painters, whom they admired, the Hague School artists like **Anton Mauve** (1838-88) and the three Maris brothers were concerned with portraying the effects of light; they were, however, more conservative than their French counterparts and it is this caution that appealed to bourgeois collectors like Burrell. During his early years as a collector he favoured the Hague School as much if not more than any other group of painters. He had a particular affection for **Matthijs Maris** (1839-1917) who had settled in London and was influenced by the Pre-Raphaelites. Burrell acquired over fifty of his paintings, drawings and prints. The choice of the ethereal, almost whimsical *Butterflies* and *The Sisters* reveals an unexpectedly sentimental side to Burrell's nature. *Butterflies* inspired him in his old age to wax lyrical on artistic matters: 'He [Matthijs Maris] was a dreamer and his pictures are poems in paint, full of feeling and tenderness . . .'.

Although **Jacob Maris** (1837-99), like his brother, had studied and worked in Paris, he was imbued with the spirit of his illustrious 17th-century fellow-countrymen. His town and harbour scenes, such as *Amsterdam*, painted about 1885, reveal his debt to the Ruysdael family, but his palette and interest in the effects of sky show his affinity with the Barbizon School and the Impressionists.

38 Matthijs Maris: *Butterflies, signed and dated 1874*   *Oil on canvas, 64·8×99·1cm (25½×39in)*   *Reg. no. 35/330*

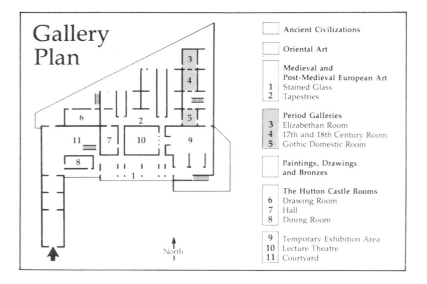

Gallery
Plan

☐	Ancient Civilizations
☐	Oriental Art
☐	**Medieval and Post-Medieval European Art**
1	Stained Glass
2	Tapestries
	Period Galleries
3	Elizabethan Room
4	17th and 18th Century Room
5	Gothic Domestic Room
☐	**Paintings, Drawings and Bronzes**
	The Hutton Castle Rooms
6	Drawing Room
7	Hall
8	Dining Room
9	Temporary Exhibition Area
10	Lecture Theatre
11	Courtyard

North

39

From the Painting Galleries the tour now goes back several centuries through a suite of three PERIOD ROOMS, created to give an impression of domestic interiors of particular eras. The first of the Period Rooms, the GOTHIC DOMESTIC ROOM, can be entered from the Hague School Gallery through the elaborate late 15th or early 16th-century doorway. The most reliable evidence we have for late medieval domestic interiors in northern Europe is provided by the paintings of Netherlandish artists such as Jan van Eyck, Rogier van der Weyden and Hans Memling; the Gothic Domestic Room contains furnishings and objects which appear in such pictures and which could have been found in the house of a well-to-do merchant or gentleman of the period *c.*1475-1525. The *oak panelling* with its frieze of Renaissance-style motifs along the end wall of the room was originally in a medieval merchant's residence in Ipswich which subsequently became a public house, the Neptune Inn. One of the two small *tapestries* in this room was also owned by a merchant: the hanging depicting *King David and Bathsheba* bears the shields of arms of Heinrich Ingold, a Strasbourg merchant in the late 15th century, and his wife Clara.

Little is known about the other large furniture items in this room but most of them must have come from domestic residences, including the Netherlandish oak *armoire* or cupboard; the Renaissance-style carved decoration with male heads dates it to the early 16th century. The openwork traceried windows on the

English *oak hutch,* or small cupboard, had a practical as well as ornamental function, for they permitted ventilation of the food stored within.

The *oak ceiling* above the Gothic Domestic Room has some fine carved bosses and other decoration. During the 19th century this excellent example of English late medieval craftsmanship was installed in a coffee-house at Bridgwater, Somerset. This was not its original location, for it was cut down to fit the coffee-house and it is likely that it previously formed part of the roof of a church in the neighbourhood. The *Bridgwater Ceiling* has been placed in a domestic setting in the gallery as it resembles timber ceilings in houses like that owned by Thomas Paycocke at Great Coggeshall in Essex. Amongst the bosses is a Tudor rose surmounted by a crown and the boar device of Richard III, which point to a late 15th-century date.

The two recessed showcases contain a variety of *domestic utensils,* including large brass plates manufactured in Nuremberg, bronze candlesticks, a ewer and a bronze chafing dish used to warm food. Amongst the more luxurious items is a German late 15th-century *drinking horn* with silver-gilt mounts and a fine group of popular medieval drinking vessels, known as *mazers.*

Even in private houses religion was ever-present. In northern Europe most if not all of the domestic residences of the well-to-do had small altarpieces for private devotional use. The *altarpiece* displayed in one of the cases is an example of a type known to have been used in English late medieval houses. It consists of an

40

40 Mazer Bowl   *English, c.1500   Maplewood and silver-gilt, diameter 25·4cm (10in)   Reg. no. 43/62*

39 *The Gothic Domestic Room with the Bridgwater Ceiling. Photograph by Keith Gibson*

alabaster panel carved with the head of St John the Baptist on a
plate which is surrounded by the figures of saints whose names are
painted along with other devices on the inside of the two oak wings
or leaves.

41 *The Seventeenth and Eighteenth-century Room showing the English bureau cabinet
and, on the end wall, the Portrait of a Gentleman by* Frans Hals. *Photograph by
Keith Gibson*

41   The SEVENTEENTH AND EIGHTEENTH-CENTURY ROOM is
reached from the Gothic Domestic Room via the Prints and
Drawings Gallery. Hanging on the west and south walls is a
selection of 17th-century Dutch pictures, of which pride of place
42 goes to the **Rembrandt** *Self-Portrait*. The precision of the church
interiors by **Hendrick Cornelisz van Vliet** (1611/12-75) may be
compared with Bosboom's more impressionist treatment of the
same subject in the Prints and Drawings Gallery. Holland in the
17th century was at the height of its power and prosperity, based
on the entrepreneurial skills of the city and town burghers who
were the main patrons of the painters. *Jacob Trip* was a merchant of
Dordrecht whose forbidding portrait painted in 1657 by **Nicolaes
Maes** (1634-93) captures the stern Calvinistic nature of the Dutch
burghers. Maes was a follower of Rembrandt, who also painted
portraits of Trip and his wife. The *Portrait of a Gentleman by* **Frans**

42 Rembrandt van Rijn: *Self Portrait, signed and dated 1632. Oil on panel, 63·0×47·0cm (24¾×18½ in) This painting was formerly in the French royal collection before its dispersal in 1792. Reg. no. 35/600*

Hals is a freer and less austere treatment of another member of the well-to-do classes. This picture was Sir William Burrell's most expensive acquisition: it cost him £14,500 in 1948.

It is not hard to understand why Dutch 17th-century paintings appealed to Burrell's reserved, somewhat frugal nature. For the same reason the frills and fripperies of Baroque and Rococo art failed to attact him and his purchases in this field were almost entirely confined to the relatively restrained fields of British portraiture, furniture, glass and silver.

18th-century portrait painting was one of Burrell's early enthusiasms and he continued to make a few acquisitions in this field after the First World War. The most important of these was by **William Hogarth** (1696-1764), the portrait of *Mrs Ann Lloyd*. Portraits by the following artists can also usually be seen in this room: **Nathaniel Hone** (1718-84), **Sir Henry Raeburn** (1756-1823) and **George Romney** (1734-1802) (of the playwright *Richard Brinsley Sheridan*). The most eye-catching item of furniture is the *walnut bureau cabinet*, a magnificent example of the art of the English cabinetmaker. It was made in about 1705 and comes from Castle Howard in Yorkshire.

The recessed showcases at the north end of the room contain a selection of early 18th-century **English porcelain, table glass and silver**. The *Chelsea figurine* of Isabella d'Andreini and the *Bow pair* of the actress Kitty Clive and actor Henry Woodward are amongst Burrell's few gestures towards Rococo taste. The glass includes tapersticks, and wine and cordial glasses. Most of the silverware exhibited was made by London goldsmiths, although there is a *stem bowl* made in Edinburgh by **James Mitchellsone** in 1726-27. A silver-gilt *caster* hallmarked London 1710-11 also has Scottish connections in that it is engraved with the arms of the Marquess of Lothian.

Beyond the Seventeenth and Eighteenth-Century Room lies the ELIZABETHAN ROOM, containing items primarily from the reign of Queen Elizabeth I (1559-1603), along with some dating from the time of her successor James VI of Scotland and I of England: there was a strong artistic continuity during the period spanned by the two reigns. A number of the artefacts can be associated in one way or another with Queen Elizabeth herself. The large *oak fireplace* and overmantel occupying the end wall date from the late 16th century and reputedly come from the destroyed Tudor royal palace of Oatlands, near Weybridge in Surrey. This is not entirely certain, but the display of the arms of England suggests a royal connection of some kind. The elaborate carvings of caryatids, lion masks, mermaids, etc., are all part of the standard repertoire of ornament used in Elizabethan and Jacobean England. *The Kimberley Throne* is another item in this room which can be linked with Queen

43

Elizabeth. It was discovered at Kimberley Hall in Norfolk, the residence of the Wodehouse family. Traditionally it has been associated with a visit made by the Queen to Kimberley in 1578.

43 The Kimberley Throne   *English and Italian or French, 16th century   Gold and silver thread, coloured silks and applied satin on red velvet; padded work, height 336cm (11ft)   Reg. no. 14/217   Photograph by Keith Gibson*

Other items are connected with members of her Court. On the wall opposite the fireplace hangs a portrait of the great statesman *William Cecil, Lord Burghley* (1520-98), resplendent in his robes and insignia of the Order of the Garter. There are several versions of this picture, all attributed to the school of **Marcus Gheeraerts**; they were probably painted around 1585. The *tapestry* on the west wall depicts the arms and supporters of the Queen's ill-fated favourite Robert Dudley, Earl of Leicester (1532-88), and is one of a set woven in 1584-5 for the banqueting house attached to his residence in the Strand, London. The tapestries were obtained from Richard Hicks, head weaver of the Sheldon tapestry manufactory, and they are almost certainly of English origin. The late 16th-century *Jack Clock*, so named from the seated figure which strikes the quarters and hours, is one of the small group of time-pieces in the Collection; painted on the dial-plate are the arms and crest of the Avery family. The *oak table* is worth a close inspection. The elaborate inlays in lighter-coloured wood include the initials IB and MB, the arms of the Brome and Crossley families and the date 1569, all enclosed in strapwork cartouches and other Renaissance designs. There is a very similar table at Hardwick Hall in Derbyshire.

Strapwork also appears in profusion on some of the **silver** displayed in the showcases in this room, including the *communion cups*. The most elaborate pieces are the three silver-gilt *steeple cups*, so-called because of the tall pinnacles on the lids; they were made in London in 1611-12. The London goldsmiths did not have a monopoly of production in the Elizabethan and Jacobean periods. Exeter was an important centre and works by **John Jons** and **C. Eston** from that city are shown here. The latter was responsible for the mounts on a *stoneware jug* dated 1589. Not all tableware of these epochs was of silver; until the 18th century most simple household vessels were made of wood. These are known as **treen**, and there are some very good examples in the Burrell Collection. The *Hickman Chalice* and several of the other cups reveal their indebtedness to goldsmiths' designs. The sycamore *trenchers* or platters carry verses which were sung or read out by the guests whilst dining.

44

44 Communion Cups   *English, (1) hall-marked London 1576-7 (2) dated 1574 and with the maker's mark of John Jons of Exeter   Silver, height (1) 17·2cm (6⅚in) (2) 17·5cm (6⅛in)   Reg. nos. 43/9, 10*

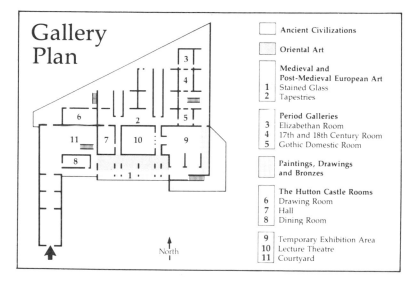

Gallery Plan

	Ancient Civilizations
	Oriental Art

Medieval and Post-Medieval European Art
1 Stained Glass
2 Tapestries

Period Galleries
3 Elizabethan Room
4 17th and 18th Century Room
5 Gothic Domestic Room

Paintings, Drawings and Bronzes

The Hutton Castle Rooms
6 Drawing Room
7 Hall
8 Dining Room

9 Temporary Exhibition Area
10 Lecture Theatre
11 Courtyard

North

The tour continues from the Elizabethan Room into the
BRONZES GALLERY. This may be reached either by passing
through the east doorway and returning down the Painting
Galleries, or by retracing one's steps back through the Period
Rooms and past the Hague School Room; the large doorway at the
south end of the last room gives access to the Bronzes Gallery. A
vista back up the Painting Galleries to the woodlands beyond is
framed majestically by the limestone portal from Montron near
Château-Thierry in eastern France. It dates from the late 12th
century and the carved decoration demonstrates the rich
imagination of the Romanesque sculptor.

Most of the bronzes in this section of the gallery are by **Auguste
Rodin** (1840-1917), and like *The Age of Bronze* and *Eve* in the
Courtyard (see p.16), they reveal his interest in the human body.
The craggy head of *Honoré de Balzac* conveys the novelist's powerful
personality; this cast is one of several studies made for the full-
length monument to Balzac commissioned in 1891 for the Palais-
Royal in Paris but never erected there; it is now in the Museum of
Modern Art, New York. Several of Rodin's bronzes in the Burrell
Collection are replicas of well-known compositions, including *Jean
d'Aire*, which is a preparatory study for one of the six figures in *The
Burghers of Calais* group. *The Thinker* is one of a number of casts for
the *Gates of Hell*, a commission which Rodin received from the
French government in 1880 for an entrance portal to the School of

45 *The Bronzes Gallery looking towards the Montron Portal.*

Decorative Arts in Paris and which remained unfinished. *The Thinker* represents the Italian poet Dante, pondering the fate of mankind; it was intended to be seen from below, so the sculptor, lengthened the arms and enlarged the shoulders to give a towering and dominating effect.

46   *The Blacksmith* and *The Gleaner* by **Constantin Meunier** (1831-1905) and **Charles van der Stappen** (1843-1910) respectively, both Belgian artists, reveal the same spirit of realism and belief in the nobility of labour as the paintings of their French contemporaries like Millet. The half-length study of *Lillian Shelley* by **Jacob Epstein** (1880-1959) is dated 1920, which makes it one of the most modern works purchased by Sir William Burrell.

There is a good view from the Bronzes Gallery down into the RESTAURANT, around which are displayed no fewer than 63 panels of 16th-century **heraldic glass**. A closer inspection can be made from the Restaurant itself, where there are two boards giving information on the glass. The panels come from three English domestic residences: *Vale Royal* in Cheshire, *Compton Verney*,

46 Constantin Meunier: *The Blacksmith*   *Belgian, c.1870-80*   *Bronze, height 48.2cm (19in)*   *Reg. no. 7/5*

47 Arms of Sir Edmund Knightley   *English, c.1530-40*   *Stained glass, 78·1×47·0cm (30¾×18½in)*   *Reg. no. 45/332*

Warwickshire, and *Fawsley Hall* in Northamptonshire. The last series was set up in the windows of the Great Hall at Fawsley, in which formal banquets were held, so the Burrell Restaurant provides a modern setting for the glass in keeping with the original location. There are 39 panels from Fawsley, most of which commemorate the ancestry of Sir Edmund Knightley (d.1542), who built the Hall, and that of his wife Ursula, sister of John de Vere, 14th Earl of Oxford. The Vale Royal series includes shields of the royal arms of England and of various powerful Tudor magnates and members of the Cheshire landed gentry. The last four panels in the south-west corner of the Restaurant come from the private chapel at Compton Verney and depict the arms of leading Midlands families in enamel painted glass.

47

48   **STAINED GLASS** is intimately associated with architecture and for this reason the wooden supports for the external glass walls of the gallery have been used as the setting for the ancient glass, not

48 *The display of medieval stained glass in the South Gallery. Photograph by Keith Gibson*

only in the Restaurant but along the entire length of the front façade of the building. As it faces south the glass is seen to best advantage and it is interesting to watch how the colours alter during the course of the day and as the seasons change. They are at their most brilliant on frosty days or with snow on the ground; during the hours of darkness the glass is artificially lit from inside so that it can be enjoyed from the park itself. In other words, the medieval glazing is seen today much as it would have appeared in its original ecclesiastical setting.

The panels, which date from the mid-13th to the early 16th century, are arranged chronologically from the corner nearest the Restaurant to the arch leading to the Hutton Dining Room and the Entrance Arm. The majority are of German origin, but they also include panels from Austria, England, France and the Netherlands. This arrangement demonstrates how glass-painting differed from region to region and how styles and colours changed over the centuries from Early and High Gothic through to the infiltration of the Renaissance into northern Europe. Several of the panels have a known provenance or can at least be ascribed to a particular area. For example, the figure of *St Jerome* comes from western France, possibly Evron. The pair of fine ornamental panels on red and blue grounds were originally in the former Augustinian church at Erfurt, in the German Democratic Republic, and the angel over the architectural canopy formed part of the glazing of the parish church at Wiener Neustadt in Austria. All these date from the first half of the 14th century. Most of the subjects represented are religious, but the twelve north German panels include scenes of daily life, such as ploughing. There are several good English 15th-century panels, especially the *Annunciation* and *Assumption of the Virgin* from Hampton Court in Herefordshire. Several come from churches in Norfolk and Suffolk, a region which had a distinctive style of glass-painting towards the end of the Middle Ages. The *St Mary Magdalene* is a typical example of the work of the Norwich glaziers.

49

49 Ploughing *North German, early 15th century   Stained glass, 68·5×49·5cm (27×19½in) Formerly in the Collection of William Randolph Hearst.   Reg. no. 45/486*

50 St Nicholas *German, Rhineland, early 16th century   Stained glass, 114·3×45·1cm (45×17¾in)   Reg. no. 45/439*

St Mary Magdalene also appears anointing Christ's feet in a late 15th-century panel from Cologne. Several contemporary Cologne panels depicting *Solomon and the Queen of Sheba*, the *Judgement of Solomon* and the *Miracle at Cana*, which are set in the adjoining bays, testify to the variety in styles that could occur amongst glass-painters even in the same city.

Almost all the ecclesiastical as opposed to domestic glass in the Burrell Collection was removed from churches and monasteries during the secularization of religious buildings and property which swept through France, the Low Countries, Germany, Austria and Switzerland in the aftermath of the French Revolution in the late 18th and early 19th centuries. This dispersal coincided with a revival of interest in the Middle Ages amongst the English upper classes and an enormous traffic in glass took place between the Continent and the British Isles, as a result of which windows in many country houses were embellished with medieval panels. The **50** *St Nicholas* panel was imported from the Netherlands and offered for sale in London and Norwich in 1804. It represents one of the miracles performed by St Nicholas, in which the three boys in the tub are restored to life.

Opposite the stained glass are some **Persian wall-tiles** set in the pillars, a foretaste of the contents of the showcases in the South Gallery. All except one are of 13th and 14th-century date and come from Kashan in Persia (Iran). The largest is the arrangement of star and cross-shaped tiles on the central pillar. These probably came from the tomb of an Islamic saint, the Imamzadeh Yahya at Veramin, south-east of Teheran. The tiles are painted in lustre which gives a metallic sheen to them. The inscriptions around the edges are taken from the Koran. On the last pillar at the Restaurant end of the South Gallery is another impressive Persian tile in the form of a twelve-pointed star, with a beautiful arabesque design in blue, turquoise, white, red and gold. It is later than the other tiles, dating from *c*.1400.

The series of showcases incorporated into the these pillars contain a selection from nearly 300 items of **ISLAMIC METALWORK AND CERAMICS**, a field in which Burrell collected seriously only in the last ten or eleven years of his life. The artefacts range in date from the 9th to the 17th centuries and come from an area stretching from modern Turkey in the west to Samarkand in the east. Those on display demonstrate the variety of techniques used by the Near Eastern potters. Some of the earliest pieces, which are in the case nearest to the Hutton Dining Room and date from the 9th and 10th centuries, are decorated by painting with coloured slip (a clay-water mixture) and then glazed. These come from Khurasan and Transoxiana, divided between modern Iran and the Soviet Union. Several vessels from the Garrus area of north-western Persia are decorated using the *sgraffito* technique, in which sections of the slip covering are removed to reveal the dark body and accentuate the decorative designs, usually human or animal.

Examples of 12th and 13th-century **Persian fritware** appear in the next five showcases. Fritware is a mixture of secondary clays and frit (a melted and then reground silicate), and a very varied decoration was applied. In two showcases are various *lustreware*

51

51 Bottle   *Persian, 12th-13th century A.D.   Fritware glazed with lustre decoration, height 35cm (13¾in)   Reg. no. 33/124*
Pilgrim Flask   *Persian, 12th-13th century A.D.   Fritware glazed and decorated with lustre, height 20·6cm (8⅛in)   Reg. no. 33/158*
Jug   *Persian, 13th century A.D.   Fritware with underglaze blue and lustre decoration, height 28cm (11in)   Formerly in the collections of I.E. Taylor and E.L. Paget. Reg. no. 33/168*

vessels decorated like the wall-tiles. The motifs on these and on other wares show that the Islamic prohibition on the representation of the human figure was not universally applied. The influence of

China was always strong on Near Eastern potters; from the Tang Dynasty (A.D. 618-907) onwards Chinese ceramics were imported into the area and imitated. Sometimes direct copies of Chinese prototypes were produced, such as the green fritware dish decorated with fishes, made in Persia in the 13th or 14th century. In the same showcase are some 17th-century *porcelains* with underglaze blue decoration similar to the pieces from the Ming and Qing Dynasties displayed in the Oriental Daylit Gallery. One bowl even has figures wearing Chinese-style clothes and placed in a landscape with pagodas.

The **Turkish pottery** industry which flourished at Iznik (ancient Nicaea) between the 15th and 17th centuries made use of both Chinese decorative designs and Islamic elements, often combined together on the same vessel. The last showcase before the Restaurant contains examples of these attractive dishes, jugs and tankards.

52 *Caucasian, Indian and Persian carpets in the South Gallery. Photograph by Keith Gibson*

The remainder of the South Gallery is devoted to a selection of **CAUCASIAN, INDIAN AND PERSIAN CARPETS** of the late 16th to 19th centuries. Most have a woollen pile, but some are silk. Amongst the earliest is the fragment of an *Indian animal carpet* displayed on the floor outside the Hutton Hall. It is the largest surviving fragment of what must have been a magnificent carpet, formerly in the collection of the Holy Roman Emperors in Vienna. It depicts a wide variety of flowers, animals and birds, both real and fantastic. Mythical beasts, this time dragons, are the chief element in the design of the large *Caucasian carpet* which hangs towards the Restaurant end of the South Gallery. This particular carpet dates from the 17th century, when the dragon designs were at their finest. The *Hunting Carpet* on the floor nearby shows a naturalistic treatment of the animal world. Large Persian carpets often had a design based on formal ornamental gardens, complete with a central pool, waterways containing fish, paths, trees and flowers. *The Wagner Garden Carpet*, which can normally be seen in the Hutton Drawing Room, is amongst the finest garden carpets in existence, and another sometimes hangs in the South Gallery. Carpets are notoriously difficult to date, as is illustrated by one of the largest in the Collection. It is named after a previous owner, Prince Alexander Dietrichstein, and traditionally is said to have been given to the Empress Maria Theresa of Austria (1717-80) by the then Shah of Persia. Recent research, however, suggests that the carpet is no earlier than the 19th century. Its splendid condition and design make it one of the most attractive carpets in the Collection.

53 Hunting Carpet   *Indian, 17th century* A.D.   *Woollen pile, cotton warps and wefts, 475×170·2cm (16ft 7in×6ft 7in)   Formerly in the collection of the Earl of Mount Edgcumbe.   Reg. no. 9/32*

54   The tour now moves to the TAPESTRY GALLERY, which can be entered by the carpeted passageway towards the eastern or Restaurant end of the Carpet Gallery. On the right side of this passageway is the TEMPORARY EXHIBITION AREA, where changing displays of various parts of the Collection can be seen. On the left is the LECTURE THEATRE, which is mainly used by the Education Staff for schools-related activities, but where film shows, seminars and talks also take place. Dates and times of such events are displayed on the Notice Board in the Courtyard. The only items from the Collection permanently displayed in the Lecture Theatre are the portraits of Burrell's mother and his sister Mary, painted by **George Henry** and **John Lavery** respectively.

The TAPESTRY GALLERY is the main area in the building for the display of some of Burrell's world-ranking collection of over 150 tapestries, ranging in date from the 14th to the early 16th century, and representing all the major centres of production in this period. Sir William Burrell always considered that the tapestries were the most valuable part of his collection. Although he bought tapestries throughout his collecting life, most of the outstanding acquisitions were made in the late 1920s and 1930s.

The space has been arranged so as to give the impression of a Great Hall in a late medieval mansion or castle, and an architectural setting is provided at the east end by the *limestone doorway* which gives access to the Gothic Domestic Room (this doorway belongs with the limestone arches in the European Daylit Gallery.) Further, the centre section and west bay are overlooked by three early 13th-century *limestone arches* which belonged to a house in Provence (see p.87). The painted *Beaudesert Screen* in the east bay, near the limestone doorway, comes from the great hall at Beaudesert in Staffordshire, a residence of the Bishops of Coventry and Lichfield before the Reformation.

The Tapestry Gallery also contains **oak furniture** and displays of weapons. The former include, in the centre section, an early 16th-century *canopied bench* with the arms of the Earl of Ormonde and a large 17th-century English *dining table*; in the west bay, near the entrance to the Hutton Hall, there is a very fine *trestle table* of *c*.1500 which originally stood in the kitchen of Durham Cathedral Priory. The **weapons** are to be found at the entrance to the two Daylit Galleries and they date from the 16th and 17th centuries. They are variously of Italian, French, German and Austrian manufacture.

54 *The Tapestry Gallery. Photograph by Alastair Hunter*

Two *spears* and a *halberd* were made in 1558 for the service of Ferdinand I, King of the Romans (later Holy Roman Emperor) and their blades bear his engraved device and initials.

About eighteen tapestries can usually be seen in the Tapestry Gallery, although this number will fluctuate as changes are made at regular intervals. The most instructive way to examine them is by beginning with the earliest, the **German and Swiss tapestries**, which hang in the east bay, next to the Gothic Domestic Room. Most are quite small and those with religious subjects were used as
55   altar frontals. *Scenes from the Life of Christ and of the Virgin* next to the Beaudesert Screen is an example of these. Below the Nativity kneels a Dominican nun, almost certainly the donor of the tapestry, which was probably woven in Basle.

German tapestry weaving never became a highly organized commercial industry, and seems to have been carried out in small workshops in convents and houses. The products are not very sophisticated but they are appealing largely because of the naivety and almost childlike simplicity of the designs, as in the *Bible Tapestry* on the wall opposite to the Beaudesert Screen. This was woven in the Middle Rhineland during the early 16th century and has thirty-four Old Testament and two New Testament scenes,

55 Tapestry: *Scenes from the Life of the Virgin and Christ (detail)*   *Swiss,
c.1450-75*   *Wool and linen, 96·5×259·1cm (38×102in)*   *Reg. no. 46/46*

representing a synopsis of Bible history from the Creation (in the upper left corner) to the birth of Christ (lower right). It is thus the medieval equivalent of the modern cartoon strip.

By no means all of the German tapestries depict religious subjects. The earliest tapestry in the entire Collection, the *fragment* woven *c.*1300 in or near Freiburg-im-Breisgau, southern Germany, which is displayed on the wall between the east bay and the European Daylit Gallery, has interlaced lozenges filled alternately with monsters and pairs of birds. Another example is the charming scene on the east wall of peasants *haymaking*. This was almost certainly part of a set of Labours of the Months and was intended to hang in a private house. The wealthy patrician families of the German cities were the main patrons of these tapestries and the owners or donors of several in the Burrell Collection are known.

The simple and direct style of some of the German tapestries is a far cry from the accomplished products of the contemporary **Netherlandish and French** weavers, examples of which can be seen in the main section and in the west bay. The well-known *Peasants Hunting Rabbits with Ferrets* in the west bay was probably woven in

56 Tapestry: *Open-air Meal in the Garden of Love   Franco-Netherlandish, early 16th century   Wool and silk, 292·7×362·0cm (9ft 7¼in×11ft 10½in)   Reg. no. 46/66*

57 Tapestry: *Hercules Initiating the Olympic Games* Franco-Burgundian, *c.*1450-75 *Wool, 386×477·5cm (12ft 8in×15ft 8in) Reg. no. 46/80*

Tournai and it is one of the finest tapestries of the period, displaying a sense of movement and naturalism together with an interest in perspective. Scenes of rustic life and pastoral feasting and dalliance were common subjects, exemplified by the *Camp of the* **56** *Gypsies* and the *Open-Air Meal in the Garden of Love*, both of which also hang in the west bay. Representations of rulers and the members of their courts appear in some tapestries. The huntsman in the *The Flight of the Heron* in the west bay bears a very strong resemblance to portraits of the French king Francis I (1515-1547), and two of the Burgundian dukes, Philip the Good (1396-1467) and his son Charles the Bold (1433-1477), can almost certainly be **57** recognized in *Hercules Initiating the Olympic Games*, displayed in the main section. *Hercules* was very probably a ducal commission and tapestries in France and the Netherlands were highly prized by rulers and their courts.

Several of the hangings can be associated with important

personalities. The *Triumph of the Virgin*, which dominates the central section, may have been commissioned by Cardinal Wolsey to hang at Hampton Court, and the *millefleurs* (see p.25) tapestry with the shield suspended from a tree was made for Gabriel Miro (hence the punning device of the mirror on the shield), physician to the French king Louis XII (d.1515) and subsequently to his daughter Claude, queen to Francis I. The Miro tapestry is particularly interesting as it shows a development of the *millefleurs* background into a more naturalistic landscape setting; also because the robes of the angels and the humanistic script of the motto in the border show the influence of the Italian Renaissance on tapestry weaving in northern Europe.

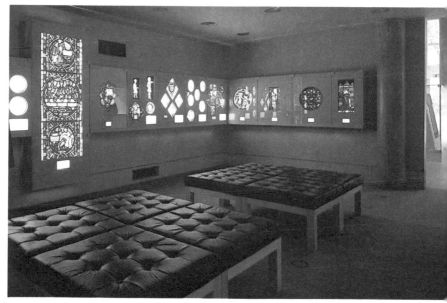

58 *The Stained Glass Room. Photograph by Keith Gibson*

Two small rooms, one devoted to stained glass and the other to needlework, can be visited from the Tapestry Gallery.

58   The STAINED GLASS ROOM, next to the central section of the Tapestry Gallery, contains some of the smaller and some of the most important items in this section of the Collection. They are artificially lit from behind and can therefore be viewed at all times. The display is also arranged at a height which allows close inspection. The rarest panel is the first on the left, depicting the

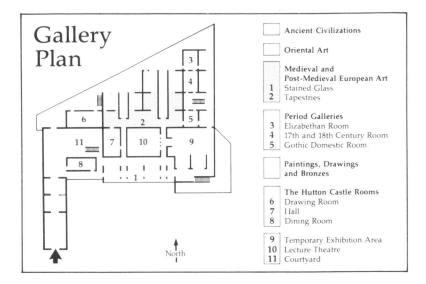

Gallery Plan

| | Ancient Civilizations |
| | Oriental Art |

Medieval and Post-Medieval European Art
1 Stained Glass
2 Tapestries

Period Galleries
3 Elizabethan Room
4 17th and 18th Century Room
5 Gothic Domestic Room

Paintings, Drawings and Bronzes

The Hutton Castle Rooms
6 Drawing Room
7 Hall
8 Dining Room

9 Temporary Exhibition Area
10 Lecture Theatre
11 Courtyard

North

Prophet Jeremiah. This is one of the earliest surviving examples of European figural as opposed to ornamental glass, for it formed part of the mid 12th-century glazing of St Denis Abbey, just outside Paris. Some 13th-century panels are displayed in the right-hand **59** section, including the figure of *Beatrix van Valkenburg*, third wife of Richard, Earl of Cornwall, son of King John and brother of Henry III. The centrepiece consists of three medallions representing *The Marriage at Cana* and the preparations for the wedding feast from a window painted in *c.*1280 for Clermont-Ferrand Cathedral in France. Amongst the outstanding examples of early 14th-century south German glass with its characteristic vibrant colours are the *Virgin* and *St John the Baptist.* From the same century but of English origin is the *Somery shield of arms,* an excellent example of heraldic art. Amongst the other English medieval shields of arms is that of *Sir Henry Fitzhugh* (d.1424) enclosed within the badge and motto of the Order of the Garter. There are several examples of the Norwich **60** School of glass-painting (see also pp.24, 65), including an *archangel blowing a trumpet.* Of considerable historical importance is the half-length figure of *Princess Cecily,* one of Edward IV's daughters. Painted around 1485, it comes from the 'Royal' window in the northwest transept of Canterbury Cathedral.

During the 15th and 16th centuries it became fashionable to place **roundels** in private houses in northern Europe. A subject frequently represented on them was the Labours of the Months,

59 Beatrix van Valkenburg   *English, late 13th century   Stained glass,*
61·0×26·7cm (24×10½ in) Formerly in the collection of Sir William Jerningham at
Costessey Hall, Norfolk.   Reg. no. 45/2

60 Archangel Blowing a Trumpet   *English, Norwich School, c.1450-1500*
Stained glass, height 39·3cm (15½ in) Formerly in the Philip Nelson Collection.
Reg. no. 45/84

and the Burrell Collection includes roundels from various sets on
this theme. The Netherlandish roundels of this period are the
finest, especially those depicting New Testament scenes and saints.
Small roundels and panels continued to be used to enliven
domestic glazing after the Reformation and particularly attractive
work was produced in Switzerland and Holland. In the former
country, representations of the standards and arms of individual
towns were common in the late 16th and early 17th centuries. There
is a good panel dated 1605 depicting a soldier holding the banner of

the town of *Zug*. In Switzerland glass-painting was often practised by several generations of the same family, and a roundel dated 1671, which is part of a series of scenes from the life of *St Francis*, is the work of **Michael Müller IV** of Zug. Dutch 17th-century roundels usually consist of simple designs, often a married couple or a shield of arms. One is of particular interest in that it depicts a slate-cutter, *Roemt Roomen*, carrying out his trade. This roundel is dated 1662. On the east wall opposite the stained glass display are three Swiss designs for stained glass. That signed by **Jacob Weber** of Winterthur is a preliminary drawing to be shown to a client for approval. The other two take the process a stage further and have the lead-lines marked in brown and the colours to be used are indicated by initials and words, e.g. *rot* for red. These drawings date from the late 16th and 17th centuries.

61 *Vista through the Beaudesert Screen in the Tapestry Gallery to the North Wall. Photograph by Keith Gibson*

The NEEDLEWORK ROOM is reached from the east bay of the
61 Tapestry Gallery via the Beaudesert Screen. A magnificent vista unfolds from the Screen through the Needlework Room, the
62 Medieval Room and the round arch at its entrance, to the glass

62 *The Needlework Room. Photograph by Keith Gibson*

63 Cap and Gloves *English, late 16th century (cap), mid 17th century (gloves)*
Cap: Coloured silks and silver-gilt thread on linen, 21×27cm (8³/₁₀×10¹/₂in)
Reg. no. 29/135
Gloves: Coloured silks and silver on leather, length 30·5cm (12in)   Reg. no. 29/139

north wall and the woodland beyond. The English late 16th and 17th-century needlework purchased by Sir William Burrell is one of the most important collections in public ownership. It is also one of the most popular sections of the Collection with visitors. It numbers more than 250 items and a representative range is exhibited in this room. Owing to conservation requirements this will be one of the displays most frequently changed.

The central showcase contains various **costume** items and accessories. The Elizabethan and Jacobean periods were the golden age of embroidered clothes, as can be seen from the *woman's jacket* of *c*.1600-25 and the various *coifs, gloves* and *caps*. The quilted silk satin *man's jacket*, and the *pair of shoes* and *cap* are typical of the much more restrained fashions that prevailed in the second half of the 17th century. Some of the items in the two recessed showcases are likely to have been the work of professional craftsmen or women. This applies to the early 17th-century *hawking set* of pouch, glove, lure and hoods (the lure and hoods seem to have belonged originally to another set). The leather pouch and glove are very delicately embroidered in silk, silver and silver-gilt threads in intricate foliage, flower and blackberry designs which are repeated on the gold and translucent enamelled mount to the pouch. The set is said to have been given in 1619 by James VI of Scotland and I of England to Sir William Pope on the occasion of a visit to the latter's residence at Wroxton Abbey, Oxfordshire. Displayed with the set are various other items of hawking equipment, including *silver bells*, a *whistle* and a *bronze hobble*. The *Purse for the Great Seal* of England is also likely to have been professionally made.

A contrast with the elaboration of the hawking set and seal purse is provided by the simplicity of the late 16th-century *communion cup veil*. The only decoration is the royal arms in the centre and Elizabeth I's titles in the borders, embroidered in silk and metal thread on linen. In the same case are various **domestic items**, including an elaborately embroidered *cushion* of *c*.1600 and *bellows* dated 1673. There are also some very attractive *cabinets* embroidered not by professionals but by young girls in well-to-do households. They contain numerous drawers, writing utensils and mirrors and they acted as a combination of vanity and writing case and jewellery and trinket box. The embroidered exteriors frequently depict Old Testament scenes: a favourite was the story of Abraham and Isaac. This was also a popular subject for **picture panels**, of which there is a selection on the west wall of the room, including examples of raised and padded work. A panel depicting *King Ahasuerus receiving Esther* (Esther II) is particularly important

63

64

because it is dated 1648 and has the arms of the Crispe family, to which it originally belonged, embroidered on the tester behind the King. Young ladies began their needlework training not with cabinets and picture panels, but with **samplers**. Samplers continued to be made well into Victorian times, but the earliest, which date from the late 16th and 17th centuries, were as the name suggests examples of different types of work and not the quaint pictures they later became. The Burrell Collection includes a fine group of 17th-century samplers displaying a variety of subjects and techniques. Some are signed and dated, including the linen sampler with raised and padded work embroidered by *Frances Cheyney* in 1664 and another, worked in coloured silks and metal thread on linen by *Jane Turner* in 1668. A further selection of needlework can be seen on the Mezzanine (see p.91).

64 Cabinet With Pastoral Scenes and Animals   *English, c.1650-1700   Coloured silks with metallic purls on satin, raised and padded work, 25·4×25·4×17·8cm (10×10×7in)   Reg. no. 29/169*

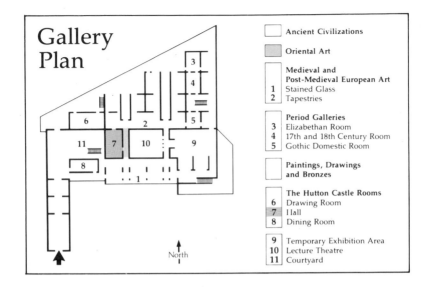

Gallery
Plan

☐	Ancient Civilizations
▨	Oriental Art

		Medieval and Post-Medieval European Art
	1	Stained Glass
	2	Tapestries

		Period Galleries
	3	Elizabethan Room
	4	17th and 18th Century Room
	5	Gothic Domestic Room

Paintings, Drawings and Bronzes

		The Hutton Castle Rooms
	6	Drawing Room
	7	Hall
	8	Dining Room

9	Temporary Exhibition Area
10	Lecture Theatre
11	Courtyard

North

Back through to the Tapestry Gallery, the next room on the
65 itinerary is the HUTTON CASTLE HALL. This can be viewed from
either of two doorways, one in the west bay of the Tapestry Gallery,
and one in the passageway linking this Gallery with the south side
of the building. The room is dominated by the *oak refectory table* in
the centre, which is more than six metres in length and bears the
date 1581. The **needlework and tapestry coverings** of the armchairs
and the settee grouped around the fireplace are fine examples of
English work of the period *c.*1650-1715 and may be contrasted with
the *oak chair* in 16th-century style (probably made for Horace
Walpole in the 18th century) which entraps the unwary sitter by
means of two iron pinions concealed in the wings. This chair is
placed in the corner between the Courtyard and the Tapestry
Gallery walls.

The most charming of the tapestries in the Hall is the small *Flight
into Egypt*, next to the fireplace. This is from a long hanging woven
in the early 15th century for the Dominican nunnery of Gnadental
in Basle, Switzerland. Next to it hangs the tapestry depicting *A
Nobleman and his Lady*. Also displayed here is the third of the set of
the Beaufort-Comminges *armorial tapestries* described in the section
on the Drawing Room (see p.25). The **rugs and carpets** are Persian,
dating from the 17th to 19th centuries, and the suits of armour are
19th-century reproductions.

The windows into the Courtyard contain an impressive set of

65 *The Hutton Castle Hall looking south.*

heraldic roundels dating from the latter part of the reign of Henry VIII (1509-47) and comprising royal badges and shields of arms. Four of these roundels come from Cowick Priory in Devon.
66 Three shields have the arms of Edward VI as Prince of Wales, and one those of his parents Henry VIII and Jane Seymour. There is also some heraldic glass in the south window, but the most important contents of this window are the three large German panels depicting, from left to right, *Christ appearing to St Mary Magdalene*, the *Meeting of Joachim and Anne* (the parents of the Virgin) *at the Golden Gate*, and the *Adoration of the Magi*. They date from the late 15th and early 16th centuries.

The principal architectural feature of the room is the stone *fireplace* and chimneypiece, a composite of various elements which was installed at Hutton Castle in 1937. The original jambs of the fireplace have been replaced by modern stonework. At the top right of the *oak doorway* into the Tapestry Gallery is an amusing *vignette* of a fox, dressed as a bishop, preaching to geese from a pulpit, a favourite late medieval theme. Built into the west wall is a 14th-century stone canopy and pedestal containing a French painted limestone group of the *Virgin and Child*, dating from the middle of

66 Roundel with the Arms of Edward VI as Heir-Apparent   *English, 1537-47*
Stained glass, diameter 40·6cm (16in) Formerly in the Lucas and Radford Collections.
Reg. no. 45/185

the 15th century. Amongst the other items of **medieval sculpture** is
a bust of the *Virgin*, also in limestone and by a French carver. As
with the other two Hutton rooms, the curtains, window seats and
lampshades were made in the late 1920s and early 1930s to Sir
William Burrell's specifications.

In the passageway outside the east door to the Hall is a
continuation of the Oriental display, containing a selection of
CHINESE JADES AND BRONZES. Sir William Burrell's collection
of **jades** was mainly formed in the 1940s. It numbers only about 140
pieces, but they span a very wide date range, from the Neolithic
period to the last imperial dynasty, the Qing (A.D. 1644-1912), and
they encompass an equally wide variety of objects: ornaments,

67

weapons, items for ritual use, humans and animals, etc. Jade has always been valued by the Chinese as a very special material. In Neolithic times it was highly prized for its hardness which made it very suitable for tools and weapons – the blades of several of the exhibited halberds and axes dating from the late Shang Dynasty (13th-11th centuries B.C.) are jade. Several *pendants* from the same period are carved in the forms of birds and fish. Amongst the later jades displayed here are some very elegant *vases* and *bowls*. The markings of the original stone vie for attention with the surface decoration and shapes of these vessels.

67 Seated Mythical Animal   *Chinese, Ming Dynasty (A.D. 1368-1644)*   *Jade,*
7·6cm (3in)   Reg. no. 22/52

68 Jue (ritual vessel)   *Chinese, Shang Dynasty, 13th-11th century B.C.*   *Cast-*
bronze, 18·1cm (7⅛ in)   Reg. no. 8/15

Most of the showcases in the passageway contain **bronzes**, which appealed very much to Burrell for their patina (the colouring built up by years of burial). Indeed, although there are less than 200 Chinese bronzes in the Collection, on the whole he preferred them to ceramics. Bronzes are amongst the first items recorded in Burrell's Purchase Books and the last of them were acquired after the Second World War.

As with jade, bronze is a material which has been worked by the Chinese for centuries. The early craftsmen were renowned for the variety of elegant forms and intricate decoration they produced. Bronze items dating from as early as *c.*2300-2000 B.C. have been discovered in China, but cast-bronze objects only appeared in any number several centuries later. The bronze-caster's art reached its height during the Shang and Zhou Dynasties (16th-11th centuries B.C. and 11th-3rd centuries B.C.) and it is from these periods that most of the bronzes in the Collection date. Most of them are *vessels* used in ritual sacrifice, especially to ancestors, and were made to contain either food, water or, as in the illustrated example, wine. Many have inscriptions giving the family name of the owner or identifying the deceased person and they are usually elaborately decorated. The creative fertility of the craftsmen in demonstrated by the many different forms of the vessels displayed here.

68

Not all of the exhibited items are food or liquid receptacles. There is an interesting group of early *bells* of the Zhou Dynasty; they have no clappers and are played by striking with a bronze or wooden hammer. The Zhou and Han Dynasties also saw the production of some elegant *weapons, horse trappings* and *chariot fittings*, a selection of which is shown in one of the smaller showcases.

69 Boppard Donors   *German, Rhineland, c.1440-50   Stained glass, 55·9×74·9cm (22×29½in) Formerly in the Pückler, Spitzer and Goelet Collections.*   *Reg. no. 45/489*

70 St John the Evangelist Scenes   *French, Rouen, c.1520   Stained glass, each light 231·1×63·5cm (91×25in) Formerly in the collection of Sir William Jerningham at Costessey Hall, Norfolk.   Reg. nos. 45/390, 391, 392*

The passageway containing the Chinese Bronzes and Jades leads through into the South Gallery, at the western end of which is an early 13th-century *pointed arch*. The slightly Islamic flavour to the decoration of this arch can be explained by the proximity of its place of origin, Provence, to Spain, which was at that time still largely under Moorish control and influence. The arch belongs with those overlooking the Tapestry Gallery (see p.70).

On the other side of this arch is the Hutton Castle Dining Room, which was visited at the beginning of the tour. Outside is the majestic conclusion to the stained glass display, consisting of **medieval windows**. The sequence begins with three mid 15th-century windows from the former Carmelite church at Boppard on the Rhine in Germany. The first contains six scenes from the *Lives of the Virgin and of Christ*; below it are depictions of two donors,

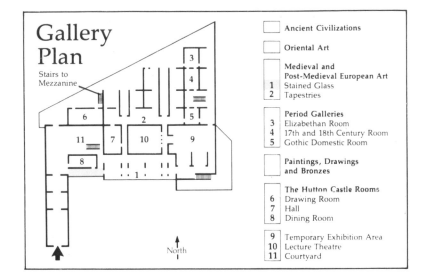

Gallery Plan

Stairs to Mezzanine

North

	Ancient Civilizations
	Oriental Art
	Medieval and Post-Medieval European Art
1	Stained Glass
2	Tapestries
	Period Galleries
3	Elizabethan Room
4	17th and 18th Century Room
5	Gothic Domestic Room
	Paintings, Drawings and Bronzes
	The Hutton Castle Rooms
6	Drawing Room
7	Hall
8	Dining Room
9	Temporary Exhibition Area
10	Lecture Theatre
11	Courtyard

69 *Siegfried von Gelnhausen* and his wife. The second, a very tall light, depicts the *Virgin and Child and the ninth commandment* ('thou shalt not bear false witness') from a Ten Commandments window. The third of the Boppard series consists of the large figures of *St Cunibert and a bishop-saint*, set under towering canopies.

The strong colours of the Boppard group contrast with the lightness of the remaining windows, which are all French. The first
70 pair depict episodes from the *Life of St John the Baptist* and, like the three-light window at the end of the sequence representing *St John the Evangelist Scenes*, appear to have come from the destroyed church of St John at Rouen. The Evangelist window was donated by the Bigars de la Londe family, who are depicted in the glass. The three windows can be attributed to followers of the Netherlandish glass-painter **Arnoult of Nijmuegen** (1470-1540), who established himself in Rouen in the early 16th century. The two panels from an incomplete *Tree of Jesse* are also from Rouen and are the work of one of Arnoult's pupils. The Jesse and the St John the Baptist and Evangelist panels all date from the early 16th century. The remaining windows outside the Dining Room comprise four 15th-century scenes from the *Life of Christ*.

At the end of the stained glass sequence is the Shop and the Entrance Arm.

71 *One of the Mezzanine Rooms. Photograph by Alastair Hunter*

71 To reach the MEZZANINE ROOMS, cross the Courtyard and go through the Hornby Portal into the North Gallery. At the end of the Ancient Civilizations section, a short staircase leads up to the Mezzanine. For visitors confined to wheelchairs or those who have difficulty with stairs, there are lifts beside the Lecture Theatre; directions to them and assistance will be provided by the gallery attendants.

The displays on the Mezzanine comprise four rooms with a pair of recessed showcases in both of the walkways above the Daylit Galleries. From this level there are excellent views down into the Tapestry Gallery and the North Gallery. The rooms are arranged in similar sequence to the ground floor, i.e. from west to east commencing with Ancient Civilizations, Oriental Art, European Medieval and Post-Medieval Decorative Arts and finally Textiles.

One of the large showcases in the **ANCIENT CIVILIZATIONS** room contains a selection of Ancient Egyptian vessels, *shawabtis* and other votive figures. There are some interesting **faience** items, including a pendant in the form of an ape and a figure of the god Bes, a household deity who gave protection to the family and its possessions. Both date from the period of the New Kingdom (*c*.1560-1085 B.C.). The central of the three large cases has some *Luristan bronzes* and other artefacts from the Ancient Near East. There is also some *pottery* and the limestone *head of a man* from Cyprus. The Roman *bronze arm* must have come from a statue of high quality. The third case is devoted to Greek, South Italian, Etruscan and Roman **bronzes, ceramics**, and **glass**. Particularly attractive are the Etruscan *bronze mirror* engraved with a winged figure and the *askos* (oil flask) in the form of a pig from south Italy.

72 The *fish plate* is from the same region. Set on most of the plinths are *Roman marble copies* of Greek sculptures of the Hellenistic period.

72 Fish Plate   *South Italian, red figure, 4th century* B.C.   *Earthenware, diameter 18·4cm (7¼in)*   *Reg. no. 19/17*

The **ORIENTAL ART** in the two recessed showcases over the Oriental Daylit Gallery and in the next room consists almost entirely of Chinese **pottery** and **porcelain**. The earliest pieces are in the northernmost of the large free-standing cases, including a Song Dynasty *bowl* still in the sagger in which it was fired in the kiln. Most of the items exhibited date from the 16th to the 18th centuries. There is a good selection of pieces with *famille verte* decoration and underglaze cobalt blue, dating from the Qing Dynasty in the Kangxi period (A.D. 1662-1722), of which there are large numbers in the Collection. Amongst the latest pieces are a *cup and saucer* and an *octagonal plate* bearing shields of arms and crests of the Haworth and Challenge families respectively. These were made for the European market during the Qianlong period (A.D. 1736-95) of the Qing Dynasty and are the only two examples of Chinese armorial porcelain in the Collection, which is rather surprising considering Sir William Burrell's interest both in heraldry and in Chinese art.

EUROPEAN DECORATIVE ARTS are displayed in the adjoining room. The 15th and 16th-century **brassware** includes several of the large dishes made in Nuremberg which bear various Old Testament scenes, saints such as Christopher and Sebastian and secular decorative designs, all in raised relief. Amongst the **bronzes** are some fine *mortars* and some interesting candlesticks, especially the 13th-century pair of *pricket candlesticks*. The third case has a display of **English drinking glasses** of the 18th century, 73 including a *commemorative wine glass*. The recessed showcase in this room and the pair in the passageway over the European Daylit Gallery contain examples of **medieval sculptures** in wood and alabaster. In common with those in the North Gallery (see pp.42-43), many of these alabasters originally formed part of English altarpieces. Most are carved with scenes from the life of Christ and the Virgin.

The last room contains **TEXTILES**, particularly needlework and lace. Owing to conservation requirements the displays here are likely to be changed fairly frequently, but usually some early 74 **samplers** and needlework **picture panels** are exhibited. The two large showcases in the centre of the room have drawers fitted with glass tops which can be pulled out. These contain some of the smaller needlework items and also a selection of **lace**, of which there are over 100 items in the Collection. This part of the Collection was formed by Lady Burrell and it includes some very fine examples in various techniques.

73 Wine Glass   *English or Irish, c.1750   Glass, height 17·2cm (6⅔ in)*
Reg. no. 15/198

74 Sampler   *English, dated 1664   Coloured silks on linen, 52·1×22·9cm*
(20½×9in) Inscribed, 'Eleszebeth Fares royght this sampler ended in the 4 day of April
1664'.   Reg. no. 31/23

The Textile Room concludes the tour of the building, with the
exception of the South Mezzanine area over the Hutton Dining
Room which houses Sir William Burrell's personal library. Some of
his rare early *printed books* and medieval *illuminated manuscripts* are
exhibited under the green cloths covering the showcases. The
South Mezzanine is not normally open to the public except at
weekends as it also contains the offices of the Burrell staff. On
weekdays arrangements can usually be made to view the
manuscripts on request at the Enquiry Desk.

BIBLIOGRAPHY

Sir William Burrell
Marks, R., *Burrell: A Portrait of a Collector*, Glasgow, 1983
Marks, R., *Sir William Burrell 1861-1958*, Glasgow Museums and Art
Galleries, revised edition 1985
The Building
Architects' Journal, 'Burrell Collection Competition', (22 March 1972)
pp.590-502, (29 March 1972) pp.642-4
Architects' Journal, 'The Burrell Collection', 178, no.42 (19 October
1983), pp.56-103
Ashley, S., 'Services to Art', *'Journal of the Chartered Institution of
Building Services*, 5, no.12 (December 1983), pp.23-26
Davey, P., 'Museum Piece', *Architects' Journal*, 177, no.6 (9 February
1983), pp.20-22
Gasson, B., 'Notes on the building for the Burrell Collection, Pollok
Park, Glasgow', *Treasures from the Burrell Collection*, Arts Council of
Great Britain, 1975, pp.117-23
Glancey, J., 'Burrell Museum, Glasgow', *Architectural Review*, 1044
(February 1984), pp.28-37
Marks, R., 'Building the Burrell', *Scottish Art Review*, XVI no.1 (May
1984), pp.3-8
The Collection
The major publications on the Collection are as follows:
Arts Council, *Treasures from the Burrell Collection*, London 1975. This
contains a comprehensive bibliography up to 1975
The Burrell Collection, with an introduction by John Julius Norwich,
London and Glasgow, 1983. This has a selected bibliography of
publications on the Collection between 1975 and 1983
The Burrell Collection: pictorial microfiche of more than 7000 items,
published by Mindata Ltd., 1983
Scottish Art Review XVI, no.1 (May 1984). This issue is entirely
devoted to the Burrell Collection
A series of leaflets on aspects of the Collection. Those so far
published comprise: *Workmen of the Pharaohs' Tombs*
Hutton Castle Rooms   *Funerary Figures of the Tang Dynasty*
Architectural Stonework   *Degas and the Dance*
The Assyrian Army   *Oak Furniture*
For Young Visitors
Scott, A., *Sam goes to the Burrell Collection*, Glasgow Museums and
Art Galleries, 1983

INDEX

Figures in **bold** denote illustrations.